Mastering The BBQ

A Compendium Of Barbecue Recipes And Knowledge

Michael H. Stines

Cape Cod Barbecue™
Cape Cod, Massachusetts

In cooperation with
Mr. Green Genes, Inc. & Tennessee Gourmet™ products
Mt. Juliet, Tennessee

Mastering The BBQ is dedicated to the
special women in my life...
Michelle and Danielle

Published by
Southside Enterprises/Cape Cod Barbecue™
Cape Cod, Massachusetts 02648-1306

In cooperation with
Tennessee Gourmet™
Mt. Juliet, Tennessee 37122-3815

For additional copies, please call (800) 360-6345
Or order online at **www.tngourmet.com**

Library of Congress Catalog Number: 2003095642
ISBN 1-932203-51-6

Edited by Jane Brooke, Toronto, Canada

Proudly printed in the United States of America
Third Printing, 2004

Barbecue Thoughts And Ramblings

Mastering The BBQ is more than a collection of barbecue and grilling recipes. Created over more than a decade from tips and recipes shared by other grill masters, backyard cooks, professional chefs, and barbecue enthusiasts, this book was written to coach, instruct, and guide a neophyte backyard cook into preparing barbecue and becoming comfortable with grilling, smoking, and barbecue. Seasoned barbecuers and veteran grill masters will find recipes, tips, and techniques to enhance and improve their barbecue and grilling sessions. An outdoor grill or offset smoker is an extension of your kitchen... everything you can do inside, you can do outside with more fun, more socialization, and better flavor!

Throughout this book, there are time-proven tips, techniques, recommendations, and suggestions to make outdoor cooking more enjoyable. Although barbecue and grilling are not difficult concepts to master, they do require patience, practice, and more practice. It also helps to have understanding family members and friends who will appreciate your efforts to learn and won't be too disappointed if your first attempts at doing 'Q turn into culinary disasters.

Cooking should be fun... whether on the top of a stove, in a professional kitchen, or in your backyard. It should be an adventure for the cook and for the palate. Fresh herbs, fresh spices, homemade stocks and sauces form the basis for good cooking whether for a formal sit-down dinner with seven courses or a backyard cookout with burgers and hot dogs.

Use the recipes and suggestions in this book to form your own barbecue and grilling favorites. Adapt the recipes to your taste buds and tolerance for heat – remember, you can always add more spice and heat but it's nearly impossible to tame a fire-breathing rub or sauce once it's on the food.

Some standards used throughout *Mastering The BBQ*...

Salt – When a recipe calls for salt, use a coarse kosher or sea salt. Coarse kosher salt has larger grains and is better suited for grilling and barbecue. It does not have the intense flavor of table salt. If you use table salt, decrease the amount by about one-third. Never use table salt for brining. The iodine content will ruin the food.

Pepper – If possible, use only freshly ground peppercorns. Pepper deteriorates quickly once ground. Invest in a good pepper mill or spice grinder and prepare ground or cracked pepper as you need it.

Herbs & Spices – Best when fresh although dried can be substituted if necessary. One tablespoon of fresh herbs equals one teaspoon of dried. In recipes calling for cilantro, use fresh whenever possible as dried cilantro tastes nothing like fresh.

Horseradish – In recipes calling for horseradish, use freshly grated when possible. If not, substitute well drained prepared horseradish in an equal measurement. Be sure to add it at the end of the cooking process as heat will minimize the flavor.

Butter – Use unsalted butter unless otherwise specified. It is easier to control the salt content and ultimate flavor of foods and sauces with unsalted butter than with salted butter. Remember, it's easy to add, difficult to remove!

Paprika – There are two types of paprika, sweet and hot. Discover the difference. Paprika should be added with fat, such as when sautéing, to release its full flavor.

Chile/Chili powder – There is a great difference. Chile powder, with an **e**, is pure ground Ancho chile (dried Poblano) while chili, with an **i**, is a combination of spices, usually chile powder, cumin, oregano, and garlic. Chili also refers to the traditional "Bowl of Red" Texas chili made with chunks of beef, beef stock, and spices. Chili con carne is Texas chili served with beans. (Real chili comes with beans on the side!)

Commercial sauces – Several recipes in this book call for using Tabasco® sauce or other Louisiana-style or cayenne pepper hot sauces. Commercial hot sauces vary in taste and range in heat from mild to nearly unbearable so substitution is not always a good idea. Other recipes call for a brand-specific sauce, mustard, or seasoning, such as Tennessee Gourmet™ Apple & Spice sauce made by Tennessee Gourmet™ or Bellycheer® Jalapeño Pepper Sauce made by Porky's Gourmet Foods. In these instances, use the specified product the first time you try a recipe. Then allow your creativity to take over and experiment with different sauces for different tastes and burn factors. Try them and have your food develop an attitude!

Cooking On The 'Barbie'... What's What

Those in the barbecue industry estimate most folks have at least five outdoor cooking sessions between Memorial Day and Labor Day. For an experienced backyard chef, outdoor cooking substitutes for indoor 12 months of the year, regardless of weather!

Barbecue is, at best, an inexact art. Different woods, varying ambient temperatures, changing weather conditions, and the food you're cooking all have to fit into the equation. The only secret in becoming a master of the barbecue is being able to produce a good meal consistently each time you cook.

Although often used interchangeably, barbecue and grilling are two completely different methods of cooking. A lot of the confusion comes from using the same piece of equipment, a barbecue grill, for both grilling and barbecue.

Barbecue, which is a noun or adjective, is a true southern method of cooking. It is rapidly spreading throughout the country. For those from the northern part of the country, barbecue usually means cooking hot dogs, steaks, hamburgers, and fish over briquettes. That's not barbecue, that's grilling.

Grilling, The Verb

Grilling is a high heat method of cooking. Food cooks directly over a heat source (coals, gas, or electric) and is normally ready in a matter of minutes. Grilling temperatures are usually in excess of 400° F. and food cooks close to the heat source. The high heat chars the surface of the food, seals in natural juices, and often creates a caramelized crust. Fat dripping on hot coals or lava rocks gives grilled food its smoky flavor similar to barbecue.

Barbecue, The Noun

Barbecue is a long, slow, indirect, low-heat method that uses smoldering logs, charcoal, or wood chunks to smoke-cook food. Barbecue temperatures are usually between 180° F. and 225° F. The addition of different types of wood chips, chunks, discs, or pellets generates smoke and the smoke gives barbecue its flavor. With offset smokers used extensively by barbecue teams across the country, the heat source is actually separate from the cooking chamber that contains the food.

Barbecue is ideally suited to large pieces of meat such as whole pigs. It is also perfect for cuts with lots of tough connective tissue like brisket, pork butts, and ribs.

More recently, a hybrid method of barbecue cooking – Indirect Grilling – has become very popular bridging the gap between barbecue and grilling. As with true barbecue, the food doesn't cook directly over the heat source but the actual cooking takes place in the same chamber, usually a kettle-type barbecue grill. Wood chips or chunks placed on the heat source generate smoke. Indirect grilling (also called covered cooking) effectively transforms a barbecue grill into an outdoor oven, which is perfect for cooking larger cuts of meat such as prime rib and turkey.

Each cooking method has its own merits. Indirect grilling gives the best of both grilling and barbecue: the charcoal flavor from grilling and the tenderness and smoky flavor from barbecue. The flavor of true barbecue is hard to beat; the trade-off is that a traditional barbecue takes a lot longer than grilling or indirect grilling.

Methods of Cooking Outdoors

All barbecue grills, regardless of their fuel source, can roast, sear, broil, spit-roast, bake, steam, and smoke foods. The following are the various methods unique to outdoor cooking:

Direct heat	Perfect for grilling and searing steaks, chops, burgers, frankfurters, fish fillets, chicken parts, or shish-ka-bobs. Use direct heat for foods that cook in less than 30 minutes.
Indirect heat	Similar to roasting, indirect heat is good for roasts, ribs, ham, whole chicken, turkey, game, or whole fish. If you're using a two- or three-burner gas-fired grill, only light one burner and place the food on the opposite side. A charcoal or wood grill should have the fuel piled on one side of the charcoal grate and the food on the opposing side of the cooking grate.
Indirect (with water pan)	An aluminum foil pan is centered between the charcoals or to one side of the heat source to regulate the temperature and to add moisture. Fill the pan with water or other liquids such as wine, juice, or stock and aromatics like onions, celery, garlic, and carrots along with herbs and spices. Don't let the pan run dry.
Pan Roasting	For large cuts of meat, pot roast, turkey, whole chicken, duck, game, or ham. Place drip pan on top of cooking grate. Add aromatics, vegetables, and wine or fruit juice. Use the liquid to baste the meat.
Smoke-Cooking	Meat, whole fish, poultry, and game take on a unique flavor when smoke-cooked. Use the water pan technique with indirect heat and wood chips soaked in hot water for an hour. Put the drained chips in a smoke box such as Sam's Smoker Pro or a heavy-duty aluminum foil packet with a few holes poked in it.

Rotisserie The meat is kept moist by its own juices when spit-roasted over low heat. The rotating spit insures all sides are done at the same time. Use a drip pan under the rotisserie to collect the drippings for basting or gravy.

Regional Barbecue Styles

While grilling is a worldwide phenomenon that began when man first discovered fire, different regions of the United States, and the world for that matter, have developed distinctive barbecue styles. Although purists argue the original four – Kansas City, Texas, the Carolinas, and Memphis – are true barbecue styles, a number of other regional differences exist.

Kansas City A big pork rib and beef brisket town. Meat is dry-rubbed then slow roasted over hickory wood. Kansas City sauces are tomato- or ketchup-based with vinegar and are sweet, thick, spicy, and commanding. Many believe Kansas City barbecue to be the best combination of all the regional styles. Kansas City also developed "burnt ends" as a delicacy. Burnt ends are the crusty, blackened end pieces of brisket that can't be sliced.

Kentucky Barbecue in Kentucky often features lamb (a sheep under 1-year-old) and mutton (sheep more than 2-years-old). Another favorite is barbecue chicken. Sauces are either a mild tomato-based sauce, a peppery hot sauce, or a unique black sauce made of a basic vinegar sauce with molasses. During cooking, a combination of Worcestershire sauce, vinegar, lemon, salt, black pepper, and water bastes the meat.

Eastern North Carolina Considered by many as the birthplace of barbecue in the United States. Usually consists of a whole pig cooked over oak or hickory wood then chopped and mixed with a vinegar-based sauce spiked with crushed red pepper flakes, black pepper, salt, and sometimes granulated sugar. The chopped pork is served on hamburger buns topped with vinegary coleslaw.

Western North Carolina Also features a pork barbecue however the meat is a Boston butt (shoulder), pulled and bathed with a thin tomato-based sauce with a strong vinegar taste. Sometimes Worcestershire sauce and molasses are added to the sauce.

South Carolina Again, "pulled" pork is the meat but the sauce is usually mustard-based with vinegar and honey or molasses. Barbecue in the Carolinas features either a creamy "Northern style" coleslaw or one made with vinegar and crushed red pepper flakes, Brunswick stew, and hush puppies (deep-fried corn meal patties).

Memphis Ribs and shredded pork dominate in Memphis. Memphis ribs come wet or dry – with or without sauce – but most come dry with a thick crust of dry rub. Western Tennessee shredded pork is mixed with a sweet tomato-based sauce, somewhat less spicy than a Texas-style sauce. Side dishes include coleslaw, potato salad, hush puppies, and baked beans. The coleslaw is usually served in the pulled pork sandwich and not on the side.

Tennessee Often called the crossroads of barbecue, nestled between Texas, Kansas City, and the Carolinas. Tennessee barbecue is mostly pulled pork cooked over hickory coals with a sweet sauce and served with vinegar-based slaw, baked beans, and corn bread. Ribs are served wet and brisket is catching on fast.

Texas Beef country! In this region, after 10 to 20 hours of slow cooking over mesquite or oak Texans have barbecue beef brisket. The sauce used is a ketchup-based blend spiked with chili powder, paprika, and cumin, limited only by what's in the pantry. Other Texas specialties include ribs, turkey, pork shoulder, and sausage. Side dishes include potato salad, coleslaw, pinto beans, and corn on the cob.

Choosing The Right Grill To Purchase

What Do You Need?

Like most appliances, barbecue grills range in price from very inexpensive (a $20 hibachi) to very expensive (a $20,000-plus state-of-the-art all stainless steel propane or natural gas grill). The more you spend, the fancier the grill and, more importantly, the higher the quality. Although you don't need a fancy barbecue grill to do a respectable barbecue, investing more money will get you a higher quality and longer-lasting grill.

Various methods of cooking: vertical smoker, deep fryer, & propane grill
(Courtesy DiversiTech)

Industry representatives say about half of all grills sold in this country use charcoal or lump hardwood as a fuel. The majority of the rest use propane while a small percentage use natural gas.

Before heading to the store, think about these considerations:

Consider **space**. If you have a large backyard, think family size grill. If you're using your balcony, the decision has already been made: get the smallest one possible. By the way, it's illegal to grill on a fire escape.

Consider the **number of people** you cook for regularly.

Figure out the **portions** of food you will cook on your grill. If you regularly host large gatherings or cook larger portions at one time, you'll need a large grill area. If you're more of a burger-and-dogs type backyard cook, think standard.

Look at the size of the grill's "primary" **cooking area**, expressed in square inches. Grills with similar exterior dimensions may have cooking areas of different sizes. Don't be confused by "total" cooking area and "primary" cooking area. The total area includes any warming racks the grill may have and does not represent the actual size of the cooking grate.

If you plan to cook large items such as Thanksgiving turkeys or primal meat cuts, note the **height** of the lid and how much room there is between the cooking grates and the top.

Take into account the usefulness of side **shelves**. They will usually cost extra, but you'll find them convenient to have a place to hold the food, utensils, and seasonings. Front shelving is also helpful but be sure it doesn't interfere with reaching the cooking grate.

Decide **how often** you'll use the grill. If you're just planning on a Fourth of July fiesta and a Labor Day bash, buy an inexpensive model. But if you anticipate holding regular cookouts throughout the year, invest in a better grill.

Don't forget to ask about the amount of **assembly** required.

Some grills have built-in **thermometers** that may or may not be accurate. It's always a good idea to purchase a meat thermometer; a popular model has a remote probe that allows the temperature gauge to be outside the grill so the lid can remain closed to stabilize the heat. Another remote probe model has a radio transmitter that sends the temperature reading to a portable digital display.

Grill Types To Consider

Once you've thought through all the considerations and your personal desires, head to a store that *specializes* in barbecue grills and accessories, and look at the three basic types of barbecue grills:

Charcoal

Charcoal grills are for the hardcore backyard chef. They give food an authentic, wood-fired smoke taste but require a lot of attention and effort.

With a charcoal grill, you build your own fire. After lighting the charcoal, the heat is regulated by adjusting the air vents above and below the firebox.

Kettle-style charcoal grill
(Courtesy DiversiTech)

Make sure the grill has adjustable vents both above the cooking surface and in the firebox so you can control airflow to regulate temperature.

Since you have to go through a bit of a "Chinese Tea Ceremony" lighting the coals and waiting for the grill to heat up, charcoal grills take longer to cook a meal than gas-fired or electric grills.

How easily can you refuel? Some grills have a hinged cooking grate that allows you to refill charcoal or add wood chips without needing to remove the cooking grate.

Propane or Natural Gas

The grill's heat is controlled by a dial making temperature regulation easier than with a charcoal grill. Although dependent on gas as a fuel source, gas-fired grills actually cook by heating

Broilmaster P3 grill

lava rocks or porcelain briquettes that transfer the heat to the cooking surface. The briquettes also help to add the "barbecue" flavor to the food by vaporizing drippings, similar to charcoal grills.

These grills cook by using propane or natural gas. If you purchase a natural gas grill, a licensed gas fitter must pipe a gas outlet to an area near your grill and you'll be restricted where you can cook (usually 12 feet from the outlet). A propane grill tank needs to be refilled periodically. A grill-size propane tank (referred to as a 20-pound tank) will last 15 to 20 hours, depending on the British Thermal Units (BTUs) produced by the grill.

Generally speaking, a 30,000 BTU grill, run at full steam, burns about 1.4 pounds of propane an hour (one gallon of propane weighs about 4.24 pounds) giving about 15 hours of grilling time. A 20,000 BTU grill burns about 0.9 pounds per hour, which equates to 22 hours of cooking time. A 10,000 BTU burner uses about one-half pound of propane an hour resulting in 40 hours of use from a single tank. Of course, most backyard chefs don't run their grills on high all the time so judge accordingly.

As an idea of what's what with BTUs: To bring one gallon of water to a boil in a 12-inch diameter pot takes less than three minutes with a 75,000-BTU burner, about seven to eight minutes with a 30,000-BTU unit, and about 16 to 19 minutes on a conventional home stove.

Purchase a gas-fired grill with two or more burners, ideally side by side, since you'll want an even distribution of heat and the ability to cook with indirect heat.

Burner quality matters more than the actual number of BTUs. Higher-quality grills have deflection devices over the burners to ensure even heat distribution and use stainless steel for the actual burners.

Many gas-fired grills offer auxiliary "side burners" for the preparation of side dishes or to keep mops and sauces warm. Most side burners produce between 11,000 and 15,000 BTUs. Although a side burner will add between $100 and $200 to the purchase price, it is a nice accessory.

Portable

Portable grills are ideal for city dwellers with small yards. Purchase a portable grill for one reason only – because it is portable. Although some portable grills look like smaller models of larger kettle grills, it is difficult to achieve similar barbecue results. For the most part, all a portable grill will allow is simple grilling... but if that is your only option, cooking on a portable grill is better than not grilling at all! There are three main types of portable grills:

Hibachis Perfect for tailgaters and beach goers, hibachis are mini charcoal grills that are easily carried. If you want to cook outside but don't have a lot of space, hibachis are a good choice for grilling although you will be limited to the amount of food you can cook at one time. Hibachis cannot be used to make barbecue.

Small Kettle Grills A smaller version of the popular Weber One-Touch® Kettle. The small kettle is only 14½ inches across and is adequate for small cooking jobs such as steaks or burgers. It is also possible to do a very small barbecue using a small kettle-style grill.

Electric grills They're small and relatively easy to operate... they are plug-in burners that preheat in about 10 minutes. Not suitable for barbecue but can be used for grilling. Obviously, electric grills need a source of power so they're not truly portable.

Dedicated Smokers

Dedicated "bullet" smokers, either "dry" or "water," are becoming a popular adjunct to backyard grills. Both types work on the same principle: a heat source (traditionally charcoal but also electric or gas-fired) heats wood chips or chunks to produce smoke and flavor food held on the higher racks.

A water smoker adds a water bowl between the heat source and the food allowing a backyard chef to add liquids, herbs, and seasonings to enhance further the flavor of the food. The water bowl also acts as a regulator limiting the temperature at the top of the smoker.

Smokers also come in a variety of styles, from the "bullet" vertical smoker to large iron and steel rigs with offset fireboxes and a cooking area large enough to roast an entire pig or smoke a dozen

Bullet smoker on a DiversiTech grill pad

9

or so briskets at the same time. Most backyard chefs don't need the large, offset firebox horizontal smoker commonly used by competition teams but smaller vertical and offset smokers are great tools for barbecue.

Most vertical smokers can also be used as open grills when the top sections are removed, adding versatility to your purchase. Expect to pay from $200 to $450 for a good-quality vertical smoker while horizontal smokers can range from a few hundred dollars to $45,000 or more for a trailer-mounted competition rig capable of cooking for 800 to 1,000 guests.

Barbecue & Grilling Tips

Whether you barbecue or grill, here are some tips to make backyard cooking more enjoyable:

Have Enough Fuel All too often backyard cooks will run out of propane or charcoal before the food is cooked! The simple solution is to have another bag of charcoal or a back-up propane tank ready for use. A 22½-inch kettle grill needs about 50 coals (one chimney's worth) for direct cooking. For indirect cooking, figure on using about 25 coals for the first hour and an additional 16 coals (eight per side) each hour thereafter. When direct cooking on a propane-fired grill, make sure the tank is at least one-half full before you begin. (The tank should weigh more than 28 pounds.)

Be Structured Professional chefs call it *"mis en place,"* having everything ready before you begin cooking. For barbecue and grilling, it means having all your utensils, sauces, and foods prepared and with you before you begin cooking. A side table makes frequent trips inside unnecessary.

Preheat The Grill Initial grilling needs to be done over high heat to sear meats. When using charcoal, let it burn until a thin coat of gray ash covers the charcoal. It's ready when you hold your hand about six inches above the grate and two seconds later the heat forces you to move your hand away. When using a gas-fired grill, preheat on high for 10 to 15 minutes with the cover closed.

Clean The Grill Grates Dirty grill grates cause food to stick. Worse, dirty grates often transfer bits of old burned food to whatever you're cooking. After you pre-heat the grill, clean the grates with a brass-bristle brush before you put any fresh food on it.

After you finish cooking and everything has cooled, clean the inside of the cover and empty the firebox. Use a wire brush and a putty knife. To minimize corrosion from acidic charcoal ashes, remove all coals and any liquids left over in the smoker or grill after it has cooled. Be sure to put the coals in a fireproof container.

Grease The Cooking Grate Oil the cooking grate just before placing the food on it. Lightly soak a paper towel with olive or vegetable oil and use a set of long-handled tongs to wipe the grates.

Soak Skewers If you use bamboo skewers for kabobs or satays, be sure to soak them in water or wine for at least 30 minutes so they don't burn once they're on the grill.

Use Tongs One of the most useful tools for grilling is a pair of long (16 inches or so) stainless steel tongs. Tongs eliminate scraping any burnt food from the grate. Don't use a fork to turn meat. Once you've pierced the meat, the juices will trickle out and dry out the meat. Juices escaping from the meat will also cause flare-ups.

Wait To Baste If you use a sugar or tomato-based sauce, apply it 10 to 15 minutes before the meat is finished otherwise the sauce will burn. Bastes or mops without sugar or tomatoes may be used from the beginning to end.

Lower The Lid Large cuts of meat and poultry cook best by using the indirect method of cooking. Keep the grill tightly covered to even out the temperature. Use a remote-reading thermometer to monitor the temperature at the cooking grate so you don't have to keep opening the lid to check on the food.

Don't Be In A Hurry Anything you cook on the grill, or inside for that matter, will taste better and be juicier if you let it rest five to 10 minutes before carving. This allows the juices that have been forced into the center of the meat by cooking to redistribute throughout the meat.

Easy With The Knife Leave some fat on the meat when grilling and most of it on when smoking or doing barbecue. The fat moistens and bastes the meat. Score the edges of steaks and chops to prevent curling.

Add Wood Even if you use charcoal or gas to cook, adding pre-soaked and drained wood chips or a handful of fresh herbs (such as rosemary) will produce aromatic smoke that will add flavor to the food. For quick grilling, use drained wood chips and add them just before cooking and after the charcoal has burned down. Be sure to soak the chips in water for at least 30 minutes so the chips smoke and don't rapidly burn. If you use a gas-fired grill, wrap the drained chips in heavy-duty aluminum foil poked with holes to keep the ashes from clogging the gas jets or use a smoking tray such as Sam's Smoker Pro.

Storing Sauces Don't store tomato-based sauces in plastic containers. The acidic tomatoes will discolor the container and make stains that are nearly impossible to remove. For serving a variety of sauces (spicy, hot, mild, etc.) at a barbecue or cookout, well-rinsed beer bottles make excellent containers (Corona has a clear bottle that works well.) Even better are clear Tennessee Gourmet™ metro glass bottles that have a nifty swing top. Similar bottles are often available from home brewing supply stores. Keep the six-pack case for easy handling.

Resealable Plastic Bags Ziploc® or similar resealable food storage bags make great containers for marinating small cuts of meat, seafood, or vegetables. Be sure the containers you use are intended for food service. To avoid spills in the refrigerator, put the sealed bag in a bowl to catch any leaks that may happen. Always marinate in the refrigerator, not on the counter top.

Warm The Meat Before placing food on a pre-heated grill, take it out of the refrigerator allow it to come to room temperature for about 45 minutes.

Condiments Use a muffin pan to hold condiments such as mustard, ketchup, relish, and onions.

Quick Start If you don't have a charcoal chimney, use this tip. Drill holes in the bottom and sides of a small metal pail or a large coffee can, fill the bottom with crumpled paper, and pile charcoal on top. Set the paper on fire and let the charcoal burn until it begins to turn white and embers form in the center. Use fireproof gloves or tongs to dump the charcoal onto the charcoal grate.

Some Necessary Utensils and Equipment

Make an investment in high-quality professional knives and cookware; it will make cooking and prep work a pleasure instead of a chore.

Good knives are essential… buy the best you can afford. Visit cook stores and feel the knife in your hand, feel its weight and balance. Find a knife that is comfortable for your hand. Along with a few good knives – a chef's knife, a paring knife, a boning knife, and a serrated sausage knife – invest in a sharpening steel. Use it every time before you use your knives and you'll rarely need to have them professionally sharpened.

Another investment for your kitchen is a quality, heavyweight wooden cutting board and acrylic boards for chicken, meat, and fish. Use a different board for each to avoid cross contamination. Wash acrylic boards in hot, soapy water after each use. Sanitize your wooden board with a bleach solution made from one teaspoon of household bleach and one quart of water. Sanitize your board often and treat it with mineral oil weekly.

Wooden spoons and spatulas are ideal for stirring and mixing but don't leave wooden utensils in sauces, they'll discolor and pick up the flavors. Never soak wooden utensils in soapy water and be sure they're dry before storing.

A small electric coffee grinder makes an excellent spice mill to grind fresh peppercorns and other spices. (Just don't use it for coffee after grinding spices.)

Have stainless steel ladles in various sizes – ½-cup, 1-cup, and 2-cup – they make it easier to transfer pre-measured stocks and liquids.

For cooking outdoors, you need to add a few more utensils to your culinary arsenal. Long-handled, wide spatulas, long spring-loaded tongs, and basting brushes all with heat-resistant handles will keep your hands and arms away from the heat. Well-insulated and flame-resistant gloves, a small plastic spray bottle filled with water to take care of flare-ups, and a supply of disposable aluminum broiler or casserole pans should be on hand as well as a re-mote-reading digital thermometer and an instant-read meat thermometer. A dry chemical fire extinguisher is also a prudent investment.

Smoking ribs in a gas grill can be done by using a smoker tray (right) and placing the ribs
on the opposite side of the heat source as shown in this Broilmaster P-3 grill. Note that the heat under
the ribs is off while the other burner is set to its lowest setting.

'Q Terminology...

Burnt ends The dark, crusty end pieces of a smoked brisket. Many barbecue aficionados consider them the prize pieces of the 'Q. Chewy and overcooked, but so good!

Direct cooking Cooking or grilling directly over hot coals, lava rocks, or porcelain squares.

Drip pan An aluminum pan, usually disposable, placed under meats so they do not cook directly over hot coals and often filled with aromatics and liquids.

Dry rub A dry seasoning mixture rubbed on meat or seafood before cooking to add flavor and seal in juices. Most rubs contain salt, pepper, and paprika and may include other seasonings such as cayenne pepper or granulated garlic.

Finishing sauce is never used during cooking but applied at the end of the 'Q or served on the side. Finishing sauces vary from plain vinegar with crushed red pepper flakes to elaborate concoctions with a myriad of ingredients. It should complement, rather than hide, the smoky barbecue flavor.

Indirect cooking Cooking food away from the source of heat, generally on the opposite side but sometimes between banks of coals. Indirect cooking is also called covered-cooking.

Marinades A combination of herbs, spices, and liquids (usually acidic) used to add another dimension of flavor and to tenderize meat.

Mop To use a brush or special barbecue mop to apply basting sauce on meat as it cooks. The mop sauce, used to add moisture to the meat, may be as simple as beer or apple juice or a well-seasoned mixture of vinegar, oil, Worcestershire sauce, herbs, and spices.

Pig Pickin' With this popular North Carolina ritual a whole pig is split, barbecued, and then laid out for the guests to pull apart.

Pork Shoulder is the front leg of the pig. For home barbecues, try the pork butt – a section of the shoulder that weighs between four and seven pounds.

Ribs Real barbecue ribs calls for pork ribs, not beef ribs. There are three types of pork ribs:

- **Country-style ribs** Come from the end of the pork loin and aren't really ribs but fatty pork chops with or without a bone.
- **Loin** or **Back ribs** are smaller and less meaty than Spare ribs. They are tender but they do not have the fat needed to stand up to long barbecue. Baby Backs, which come from a young pig, are good for shorter cooking times.
- **Spare ribs** come from the pig's belly. They have a good amount of meat on them, but more important, the top of this rib runs alongside the bacon. This gives Spares plenty of fat to keep them juicy during a long 'Q.

Searing Grilling meats over high heat to brown the outside and seal in the juices.

Smoke Chips or chunks of hardwood are soaked in water to prevent burning then placed over the burning coals to create smoke to flavor the food. Hickory, alder, mesquite, oak, apple, cherry, and pecan are most often used smoking woods.

Before Using A New Grill The First Time

Before using any grill or smoker for the first time, it is necessary to "season" it. Follow the manufacturer's recommendations, if any, or use this guide:

Remove the cooking grates and warming racks (if any) and wash them with soap and warm water. Rinse and dry well.

If using a gas-fired grill, light the burners, close the lid and operate the grill for 20 minutes or so on medium heat. Turn the gas off at the grill and at the tank (or the shut-off valve if using natural gas), allow the grill to cool and replace the grates.

If your choice was a charcoal grill, start a full chimney of lump charcoal and when they are covered with ash, place them in the middle of the charcoal grate, cover the grill with the vents fully open, and allow the charcoal to burn down completely. When done, remove the accumulated ash and you're ready for the season!

Broilmaster D4 grill

Smokers also need to be seasoned before their first use to allow the unit to settle and remove the "new" smell.

With a vertical gas-fired smoker, light the burner and bring the temperature up to about 200° F. to 250° F. Place a few pre-soaked wood chunks on the flame disk and run the smoker without any food or water for three to four hours. The routine is the same for a charcoal smoker but you'll need to replenish the charcoal supply after an hour or so to maintain the temperature.

Be sure to check all the gas fittings and connections each time you use a gas-fired grill or smoker to be sure there are no leaks. Use a soap solution on the fittings. If no bubbles appear when the gas is turned on, you're good to go!

Preparing The Grill & The Food

For best results when doing a barbecue or grilling, carefully prepare the grill or smoker before you begin cooking.

First things first: clean the grill grates. Before lighting the grill, clean the cooking grate with a brass-bristle brush. If you use a gas-fired grill, cook-off any residue by lighting the grill, closing the lid, and use the high heat to burn any residue into ash that can then be easily removed with the brush.

Another cleaning method is to cover three-fourths of the lava stones or porcelain squares with a layer of heavy-duty aluminum foil, light the grill, and allow the heat to bake off any collected residue. After the stones or squares are clean, carefully remove the foil and place it on top of the grill grates. Repeat the procedure to clean the grates.

Lighting The Grill

Charcoal or Wood Grills

The process of lighting charcoal or wood-burning grills or smokers fascinates many people as an experienced backyard chef often produces a magnificent fire with minimal effort. For others, it's a chore to avoid!

First, choose your fuel. Different fuels burn at different rates and will produce varying amounts of heat.

Wood – Cook with wood pieces or wood chips. Wood chips have more surface area than sticks or logs and will burn faster. Chips should be soaked in hot water for 30 to 60 minutes before being put on the fire so they smolder and don't ignite into flames.

Charcoal – The staple heat source for most backyard chefs. You can purchase lump charcoal (made from whole pieces of wood), natural briquettes (made from pulverized charcoal and natural starches), or composite briquettes (with sawdust, coal, and fillers). Use lump charcoal. Composite briquettes often contain borax to bind them, nitrate to make them light, and limestone to turn them

Weber kettle grill with chimney starter & grill pad
(Courtesy DiversiTech)

white... all things you don't want in your food. Hardwood lump charcoal will also burn hotter than briquettes often by as much as 200 degrees.

Don't economize when you buy charcoal. Buy high-quality lump charcoal or natural briquettes. If the charcoal contains petroleum by-products (check the label) don't buy it or your food will taste the same. For long smoking times, manufacturers caution not to use quick-lighting briquettes because of the taste they will impart to the food.

Start the fire – The easiest method is to use a chimney fire starter, a small metal cylinder with a wooden handle. Place wadded newspaper in the bottom and charcoal or wood above the paper; set the chimney on the charcoal grate and light the paper. When the charcoals have formed a gray ash coating, carefully pour them into the grill.

Or use an electric starter to light the charcoal. Electric starters are horseshoe-shaped metal loops attached to a long handle. Put the loop in the middle of a pyramid of charcoal and plug in the starter. It heats up and ignites the charcoal.

Gas-Fired Grills

One benefit of a gas-fired grill is the ease of starting the fire. Read the manual before attempting to light a gas-fired grill. If lit incorrectly, a gas-fired grill can burn you and possibly cause an explosion. Always make sure the grill is placed in a well-ventilated area, out in the open, away from the house, and away from low-hanging tree branches. Never use any grill, gas-fired, electric, or charcoal, inside an enclosed area like a garage or shed.

If using propane as your fuel, be sure to have enough to complete the cooking. A standard grill tank weighs about 39 pounds and holds 4.7 gallons (20 pounds) of propane when full. Most grills, at full tilt, will burn about two pounds of propane an hour.

Before lighting, check the gas connection, hose, and the burners for damage. Be sure the venturi between the gas valves and the burner is clear of obstructions. Spiders like to build webs inside the venturi that could cause a "flashback" when the burner ignites.

Open the lid of the grill. Turn on the gas at the source. Turn on one gas burner and ignite the gas. Most gas grills come with igniters that create a spark to ignite the gas vapor. If the igniter does not work after a couple of tries, turn off the gas, leave the cover open, and wait five minutes before trying again.

For safety's sake (and to keep your eyebrows), don't lean over a gas grill when lighting the burners.

17

How Hot Is Hot?

The major cause of gas-fired grill cooking failures is too much heat. There are three basic settings for a gas-fired grill:

High – Used primarily to preheat and for cleaning. It may also be used to sear meats such as steaks and chops quickly. Rarely, if ever, should high heat be used for extended cooking. The surface temperature at the cooking grate is approximately 550° F. on the high setting.

Medium – Used for broiling or quickly cooking food. Medium is also used for searing foods that have been cooked on low. The surface temperature is about 450° F. Useful for most grilling and baking. Medium is also good for cooking hamburgers and vegetables.

Low – Most foods should cook on low. Thick steaks that have been seared on high will finish cooking better on low. Low should be used for all roasts, poultry, rotisserie, and smoke cooking. The temperature on low is about 325° F. with two burners operating. With only one burner of a two-burner grill lit, the temperature can be maintained as low as 200° F.

For best results, you want to bring a grill to the proper temperature before putting food onto it. The temperature will vary depending on what you intend to cook. There are several options for measuring temperature:

Thermometers Many grills come with built-in thermometers (often just indicators for high – medium – low) or a pre-drilled hole that permits you to install a dial-type thermometer. The built-in thermometer measures the temperature at the thermometer probe, not at the grill surface. Temperatures at the cooking grate, and the internal temperature of the meat, will often differ by quite a bit.

The Coal Method Red hot: strongly glow red and have their highest temperature (around 425° F.); Medium hot: coals start to burn down and have a coating of ash, but still glow (around 350° F. to 375° F.); Medium Low: a layer of ash completely covers the coals, which don't exhibit red (around 200° F. to 300° F.).

The Palm Method requires you to place your hand, palm down, slightly above the cooking grate of a charcoal grill. Lower your hand slowly to test the heat! Place your hand, palm side down, about three inches from the cooking grate and count:

Time	Best Used For	Temperature
Six seconds	Indirect Smoking	Low fire
Five seconds	Covered cooking	Medium-low fire (200° F. – 300° F.)
Three to four seconds	Grilling	Medium fire (300° F. – 350° F.)
Two seconds	Grilling	Medium-hot fire (350° F. – 375° F.)
One second	Searing meat and cleaning	Very hot fire

Preparing The Food

Arrange foods on the grill so uncooked meats don't touch vegetables or other items that won't stay on the grill for very long. If you have more food than space, you can cook in batches but coordinate the entrées with your side dishes so there's something for everyone to eat while you finish cooking.

Different types of food, and the same food of different thicknesses, will cook at different rates. Start with the items that will take longer, setting them to one side, then grilling the quick-cooking items, and then finishing up with the slow-cooking item.

Seasoned backyard chefs always check their tools before beginning a 'Q or grilling session: a thermometer, a clock or timer, a long-handled spatula with a wide blade, a long-handled pair of tongs, heat-resistant gloves, a long fire-resistant apron, and a plastic spray bottle filled with water to douse flare-ups.

If cooking with wooden skewers, soak them in water well before cooking to prevent them from burning.

After Cooking: Clean-Up and More

The pleasures – and duties – of being a backyard chef don't end once you've successfully grilled, barbecued, or smoked the meal!

The Food

It keeps cooking! After you expose food to the high heat of a grill, it retains much of the heat and continues to cook after coming off the grill. If you let the food sit for too long it may become overcooked and dried out despite being taken off the grill at the proper time. Figure the internal temperature will increase five to 10 degrees as the meat rests before carving.

The Clean-Up

Once you've finished cooking and enjoying your culinary efforts, clean your gas-fired grill by closing the lid and bringing the temperature up to high for about 15 minutes to burn off any food residue. Then turn off the gas at its source, turn off the grill, and use a wire-bristle brush to scrape off the remaining residue from the cooking grates. By turning off the gas source first, vapor pressure is relieved in the gas line reducing the possibility of a leak. After the gas has burned off from the line, be sure to turn off the grill's controls.

It's easy to turn off a gas-fired grill, but charcoal or wood grillers need to take extra care to extinguish their fires. Closing the lid, the vents, and the dampers will help starve the fire of air. Be sure the fire is completely out and the coals cool before dumping any ashes into a fireproof container.

Before stopping for the day (or night), use a brass-bristle brush to clean the cooking grates. The day after, or once the grill cools, clean everything. Clean the coal grates with a stiff wire brush and remove the remaining residue with a paper towel. Don't forget to clean residues from the underside of the grill lid and from underneath the coal grates. For wood and charcoal grills, discard the coals and ashes to prevent corrosion. If left in the grill they will form an acidic compound that will eat away the firebox.

Use a heat-resistant grill cover to protect your investment from the elements.

It's also a good idea to use a protective pad such as those sold by DiversiTech to protect your deck or patio from stains.

Maintaining Your Investment

You've spent a considerable amount of money for your new grill, especially if you purchased one of the higher-priced, higher-quality gas-fired models. Maintaining your investment requires a bit of time and effort but the reward is a grill that will perform like new for years.

Routine maintenance augments the cleaning ritual you should do every time you use your grill or smoker.

For charcoal or wood grills, do these routine maintenance chores every month if you use the grill all the time or at the beginning and end of your outdoor cooking season:

- Remove the cooking grates, wash with warm, soapy water, and clean them with a non-abrasive scouring pad.

- Clean the inside of the hood with soap and water. If you do a lot of smoking in the grill, a wire brush will help remove the build-up.

- Tighten nuts, bolts, and screws.

- Empty the firebox of all accumulated ashes, brush with wire brush, and rinse with water.

- Lubricate hinges and damper/vent controls.

Gas-fired grills also need regular maintenance and, occasionally, replacement parts. (It's best to get brand-specific replacement parts and not "universal" replacements.)

Here's a checklist for keeping your gas-fired grill in top condition:

- Remove the cooking rack, cooking grates, lava stones, and grate.

- Remove the burner from the firebox. Use caution removing the burner so you don't damage it or the venturi. (There may also be a brace that needs to be unscrewed.)

- Clean the cooking grates with a wire bristle brush then wash with warm water and soap.

- Use a putty knife or wire bristle brush to remove debris from inside the firebox and the lid.

- Remove any accumulated grease from the grease tray.

- Look at the burner ports. Be sure they're not clogged with food debris or ashes. If they are, use a wooden pick or broom straw to open them. Don't use a wire probe it could damage the ports.

- Check the venturi and clean them with a venturi brush to remove any insect nests or webs. Insects have an affinity for propane.

- If you store your gas-fired grill indoors during the off-season, do not store the propane tank inside. The tank must be stored outside in a well-ventilated area.

- Every time you use your gas-fired grill be sure all the gas fittings are secure and the gas hose is free of nicks or animal gnawing. Squirrels like to chew on gas hoses.

Brining Meats and Seafood

Brining increases the moisture holding capacity of meat and fish and results in a moister food when it is cooked.

Many backyard chefs consider brining obligatory for poultry. It is also very popular when smoking various forms of meat and seafood such as salmon, pork chops, ham, bacon, corned beef, and pastrami. If you brine briskets, ribs, or pork shoulders they will all taste like ham.

Brining Times for Different Foods

Food	Brining Time
Shrimp	30 minutes
Whole Chicken (4 pounds)	8 to 12 hours
Chicken Pieces	1½ hours
Chicken Breasts	1 to 2 hours
Cornish Game Hens	2 hours
Whole Turkey	24 to 48 hours
Pork Chops	2 to 6 hours
Whole Pork Loins	1 to 3 days
Salmon Fillets	8 to 12 hours
Fish Pieces or Fillets	1" thick: 5 to 8 hours ½" thick: 4 hours Pieces: 2 to 3 hours

Brining Tips

Some people are sensitive to salt and find brined meats are too salty. To reduce the salt taste, add sugar, decrease the amount of salt, decrease the brining time, or soak the meat in fresh water for an hour before cooking.

You can brine with just kosher or sea salt and water but since salt will carry flavors as it goes into the food, add something to the mix. Sugar moderates the salty taste and helps keep meats juicy. Herbs, spices, and seasoning will also add different dimensions and flavors.

Never use table salt or iodized salt for brining, only use kosher or sea salt.

Do not overcook brined foods! Brined meats and seafood cook faster than unbrined food so be careful and use a thermometer to determine when the food is properly cooked.

Brining requires a deep food-safe container so the whole piece of meat, poultry, or fish can be submerged in the cold brine. The brine must also be kept at 40° F. or below to prevent bacteria growth. Use an ice chest or insulated cooler and cold packs to keep the brine cold. If you don't have reusable cold packs, an alternative is to put ice cubes in resealable plastic bags. If you just use ice to keep the brine cool, it will melt and reduce the strength of the brine.

If you want poultry to develop a crispy skin after brining, it needs to air-dry, refrigerated and uncovered, for eight to 12 hours before cooking.

Poultry Brine: A Spicy Variation

1 gallon cold water	1 tablespoon pickling spices
¾ cup kosher salt	1 teaspoon crushed peppercorns
½ cup white vinegar	1 teaspoon ground allspice
3 tablespoons light brown sugar	1 teaspoon granulated garlic
1 tablespoon onion powder	1 teaspoon dried tarragon leaves
1 teaspoon ground Chipotle chile	1 teaspoon crushed red pepper flakes
1 tablespoon dried rosemary	1 teaspoon dried thyme
½ teaspoon ground Ancho chile	

Bring four cups of water to simmer, add remaining ingredients, except remaining water, and stir until dissolved. Remove from heat; add remaining water. Cool before use.

Pork Brine Recipe

3 quarts water	3 bay leaves
½ cup kosher salt	1 tablespoon crushed garlic
1¼ cups granulated sugar	2 tablespoons chopped shallots
½ teaspoon ground allspice	2 teaspoons cayenne pepper sauce

Bring one quart of water to boil, add remaining ingredients, except water, and stir until dissolved. Remove from heat and add remaining water. Cool before use.

Salmon Brine Recipe

¾ cup kosher salt

1½ tablespoons crushed peppercorns

1 cup granulated sugar

1 quart water

3 tablespoons lemon juice

1 tablespoon poultry seasoning

¼ teaspoon granulated garlic

¼ cup dark molasses

2 tablespoons Worcestershire sauce

¼ cup dark brown sugar, firmly packed

3 tablespoons seasoned salt

Combine all ingredients and let stand one hour.

Add salmon, skin side up, to brine, pressing to submerge. Cover and refrigerate overnight. Remove salmon from brine and rinse under cold water. Place salmon, skin side down, on rack. Let stand about an hour until top is dry and somewhat tacky to touch (do not pat dry).

Fish Brine Recipe

½ cup granulated sugar

2 cups soy sauce

1 cup dry white wine

½ teaspoon garlic powder

½ teaspoon cayenne pepper sauce

¼ cup kosher salt

1 cup water

½ teaspoon onion powder

½ teaspoon cracked black pepper

Combine all ingredients, add fish, skin side up, and submerge. Cover and refrigerate overnight. Remove fish from brine and rinse under cold water. Place fish, skin side down, on rack. Let stand about an hour until top is dry and somewhat tacky to touch (do not pat dry).

The Right Time & Temperature

Overcooked food tastes tough and dried out; an often-heard complaint about grilled food. Undercooked food won't taste so great either and it carries the risk of serious food poisoning. There's no simple formula that will estimate the length of time necessary to grill or barbecue foods. To decide how long to leave food on the grill, consider:

- The **type of food** and its **thickness**. (A burger cooks a lot faster than a thick steak.)

- The **desired doneness**. (Medium-rare or medium-well?)

- The **heat of the grill**. Determining the amount of heat actually reaching the food becomes complicated. The temperature of the fire is higher than the heat reaching the food at the grill surface. Closed lids (and closed vents in the lid) retain more heat than open vents and uncovered grills. Wind speed, altitude, and outside air temperature all affect cooking time making outdoor cooking more of an art than a science.

And There Was Fire And It Was Good...

Because of the many factors influencing the actual time needed to cook food outdoors, knowledgeable backyard chefs use an instant-read meat thermometer to measure the temperature of the food.

For those in the northern climes, outdoor cooking need not be limited to the warmer months, but cooking during the winter does require a bit of extra preparation and work.

Some tips for cooking in less than ideal weather:

The grill or smoker will take longer to preheat when the temperature drops below 50° F. Figure at least 30 minutes for a charcoal grill or smoker and 20 minutes for a gas-fired grill to come up to temperature.

Add about 20 minutes of cooking time for every five degrees below 45° F. ambient temperature.

Add another 15 minutes of cooking time every time you open the lid to add more fuel or wood.

Outdoor cooking can be done
year-round as this photo
by Broilmaster shows

Shield the grill or smoker from the wind but don't use it in an enclosed area or under a porch overhang. Wind has a greater impact on cold weather cooking than actual temperature.

Putting a disposable turkey-size roasting pan over the cooking grates will lessen the time needed to preheat a grill in cold weather. Be careful removing the pan, it will be hot.

If you're using a drip pan, fill it with hot water. The water will help raise the grill temperature. An easy way to do this is to put the drip pan in the grill, and then add water from a tea kettle instead of trying to carry a tray filled with hot water to the grill.

Wrap a vertical bullet smoker with foil-backed insulation to keep the temperature regulated. Be sure the insulation has foil on both sides so the insulation doesn't melt.

The best foods to cook during the winter months are ones that don't need much attention: roasts, whole chickens, ribs, pork shoulders, and briskets.

Expect to use more charcoal during colder weather. To be safe, estimate on using twice as much charcoal as you would during the warmer months. Be sure to have an adequate supply on hand.

Grilling Times For Meats & Seafood

Beef				
		Rare (125° F.)	Medium (140° F.)	Well (165° F.)
New York Strip	1-inch thick	8 – 10 minutes	10 – 12 minutes	12 – 14 minutes
Rib eye	¾-inch	5 – 7 minutes	7 – 9 minutes	12 – 14 minutes
T-Bone, Porterhouse, Sirloin	1½-inches	10 – 12 minutes	12 – 15 minutes	15 – 19 minutes
Kabobs	1½-inches	6 – 8 minutes	8 – 10 minutes	10 – 12 minutes
Hamburgers	¼ pound			10 – 12 minutes
Pork				
			Medium (160° F.)	Well
Chops	¾-inch		12 – 14 minutes	14 – 19 minutes
Kabobs	1½-inches		8 – 10 minutes	12 – 14 minutes
Sirloin Roast	3 – 4 pounds		1½ hours	2 – 3 hours
Rib Crown Roast	4 – 6 pounds		1¾ – 2 hours	2 – 3 hours
Tenderloin	¾ – 1 pound		25 – 35 minutes	30 – 45 minutes
Chicken				
Boneless breast	4 – 5 ounces			10 – 14 minutes
Pieces	2 pounds			1 hour
Half chicken	1 – 1½ pounds			1 – 1½ hours
Whole	3 – 4 pounds			1¼ – 1¾ hours
	4 – 5 pounds			1¾ – 2 hours
	5 – 6 pounds			2 – 2½ hours

Grilling Times For Meats & Seafood

Turkey			
Boneless breast	2 pounds		1½ – 2 hours
Whole	6 – 8 pounds		1¼ – 2 hours
	10 – 12 pounds		2 – 3 hours
	14 – 18 pounds		3 – 4 hours
Fish			
Whole	1 pound		20 – 25 minutes
Unstuffed	1½ – 2 pounds		25 – 30 minutes
	2 – 4 pounds		30 – 50 minutes
	4 – 4½ pounds		50 – 60 minutes
Stuffed		Add 30 minutes	
Steaks	1 – 1½ inches		10 – 12 minutes
Fillets	¼ – ½ inch		4 – 6 minutes
	½ – 1 inch		6 – 10 minutes

Not Too Much Smoke Or Too Little

The use of different woods, either chunks, discs, pellets, or chips gives unique flavors and another dimension of taste to barbecue meats and seafood. Smoke makes barbecue, without it, you're grilling food.

With a charcoal grill, simply soak the chips in water or wine for about 30 to 60 minutes, drain, and place atop the coals. For a gas-fired grill, place the chips in a smoker tray or in a foil packet with a few holes poked in it and then on the lava rocks.

Another smoking choice has recently come about to the barbecue world: wood pellets. Pellets are made from dehydrated wood, sterilized, and formed into small pellets, much like rabbit food pellets, about an inch long and ¼-inch in diameter. Because of their small size, pellets burn very cleanly and have very low residue. Pellets give a much more intense smoke flavor

A 20-inch by 42-inch charcoal smoker manufactured by BBQ Pits by Klose

than chips or chunks and most smoking can be done with about one-third of a cup of pellets.

27

Sam's Smoker Pro smoker tray

Another innovative product has been produced by two engineers that makes smoking in a gas, electric, or charcoal grill much easier. Their stainless steel smoker tray is a large radiant heat deflector with top and bottom perforated plates. The offset holes create a draft and maximize smoke production while reducing the amount of wood chips needed to smoke-cook food. An accessory tray allows the unit to burn pellets.

Whatever wood you decide to use, it's best to start with a small amount to see how you like the flavor then add more for a stronger taste but be careful not to overpower the food with smoke. Too much smoke can make food taste bitter, especially with the stronger woods like mesquite. Varying the mix by combining different woods will also give smoked foods a unique flavor.

Although oak, hickory, and mesquite are the most popular woods used for smoking, with hickory being favored in the South and Midwest and mesquite in Texas, other woods are readily available as pellets, chips, chunks, and logs. Only use hard woods for smoking, soft woods such as pine or spruce will give a tar-like taste to food because of their resin content.

A vertical smoker filled with soaked and drained wood chips

The following table suggests various woods that complement smoked food:

Wood	Food	Description
Alder	Fish, Poultry, Pork, light meat Game birds (traditionally used in the Northwest to smoke salmon)	Produces the least heat; sweet, delicate flavor
Apple	Pork chops, Ham, Poultry, Sausage, Vegetables	Denser than alder; sweet, fruity smoke
Cherry	Good with all meat and fish	Sweet, fruity smoke that darkens meat
Grapevines	Beef, Lamb, Pork, Sausages, Vegetables	Tart, rich, aromatic
Hickory	Beef, Pork, Poultry, Game, Cheeses, Ribs, Burgers, Lamb	Bacon-like flavor; most commonly used wood by competition teams; adds a strong flavor
Maple	Cheese, Pork, Poultry, Game, Vegetables	Smokey, mellow, and slightly sweet
Mesquite	Beef, Pork, Poultry, Game, Vegetables	Spicy, distinct smoke; burns hot, good for quick grilling, not long barbecue; one of the strongest woods
Mulberry	Beef, Pork, Ham, Poultry, Game Birds	Sweet, tangy, apple-like flavor
Oak	Beef, Lamb, Sausage, Game birds	Heavy smoke with no aftertaste; very popular
Orange	Pork, Poultry, Fish, Game Birds, Cheese	Tangy citrus smoke; gives food a caramel color
Pecan	Lamb, Pork, Turkey, Fish, Steaks, Game, Cheeses	Nutty and sweet with a mild aftertaste; a subtler version of hickory

Sassafras	Beef, Pork	Musky, sweet smoke; mild and tangy
Seaweed (Rockweed)	Lobster, Crab, Shrimp, Clams, Mussels, Oysters	Smoky, tangy flavor; traditional for clambakes
Sugar Maple	Pork, Ham, Poultry, Cheese, Game Birds	Mild, sweet, light smoke

Smoking Times For Meats & Seafood

Food	Weight (pounds)	Charcoal (pounds)	Chips (cups)	Time (hours)
Beef				
Whole roast	3 – 4	5 – 7	2	2½ – 3½
Pot roast	4 – 5	7 – 8	2 – 3	3 – 4
Short ribs	3 – 4	5 – 7	2	1½ – 2½
Brisket	3 – 4	7 – 8	3	6½ – 7½
	5 – 7	8 – 10	3	8 – 10
Pork				
Roast, bone-in	3 – 4	8	2	3½ – 4½
	5 – 7	8	3	5 – 7
Roast, boneless	3 – 5	10	3	3½ – 5½
Spare ribs	4 – 6	8 – 10	3	5 – 7
Country ribs	4 – 6	7 – 10	3	5 – 8
Baby Back ribs	2 – 3	5 – 7	2	4 – 5
Chops, one-inch		5 – 7	3	2 – 3
Poultry				
Chicken breasts				1½ – 2
Boneless breast				1 – 1½
Chicken, whole	2 – 3	5 – 7	2	3½ - 4½
Turkey	8 – 10	8	3	4 – 6
	11 – 13	8 – 10	3	6 – 7½
	14 – 16	10 – 12	4	7 – 8
Game birds	1	5 – 7	2	2 – 3
Seafood				
Whole fish	4 – 6	7	2 – 3	2 – 3
Fillets		5	1 – 2	1½ – 2½
Shrimp		5	1 – 2	¼ – ½
Crab legs		5	1 – 2	1 – 2

Food Handling... Better Safe Than Sorry

Cooking great barbecue is a learned skill... enough practice will make anyone a great barbecue or grill chef. Food safety is a topic that must be learned and carefully practiced whenever combining food, hot temperatures, and outdoor cooking.

Much more information about food safety, safe cooking techniques, and proper storage and handling methods is available at *foodsafety.gov*.

Here are some of the basic food handling and preparation safety tips:

Thaw Properly Thaw foods in a refrigerator, not on the counter top. If absolutely necessary, thaw pre-packaged food by soaking in cold water, changing the water every 30 minutes.

Keep It Clean Wash hands for at least 30 seconds with soap and water before and after handling uncooked meat and poultry. Sanitize cutting boards and knives with a bleach solution. After cutting raw meats, wash hands, cutting boards, utensils, and counter tops with hot soapy water followed by a bleach solution. Use different cutting boards for different products – one for red meats, one for poultry, one for vegetables, and one for fish.

Don't Cross Contaminate Keep uncooked meats, fish, and poultry away from other cooked or uncooked foods. Never put cooked foods on a plate used for raw meats. Don't re-use a marinade unless it's brought to a boil to kill any bacteria. Don't use the same tongs or utensils for uncooked and cooked foods.

Cook Properly Be sure to cook food to the correct internal temperature. Use an instant-read meat thermometer to assure the food is properly cooked.

Refrigerate Promptly Refrigerate or freeze perishables, prepared foods, and leftovers within two hours of cooking. Always marinate meat and fish in the refrigerator. In hot weather above 90° F., foods should not remain unrefrigerated for more than one hour.

Keep Hot Food Hot, Cold Food Cold Use an insulated cooler to keep foods below 40° F. or above 140° F. Keep perishable foods such as meat, poultry, and fresh vegetables below 40° F. until they are ready to be cooked or prepared.

Keep It Covered Keep uncooked, cooked, and prepared foods covered as much of the time as possible. Use foil or food film on containers without lids.

Don't Reuse Never reuse raw material containers, such as poultry or meat boxes or vegetable containers, for holding cooked foods.

Use Gloves Don't handle food if you have cuts or sores on your hands. Cover open cuts with a bandage and use disposable food-grade gloves. Change your gloves when you change food items.

When In Doubt... Throw it out. If food doesn't look or smell right, don't risk food poisoning. Throwing away questionable food is better than paying for a doctor's visit. Discard any foods left out longer than two hours.

Barbecue Style: Low And Slow Cooking

One of the true barbecue "secrets" is developing a heavy smoke and cooking meat at a low temperature allowing it to tenderize. A popular method is to use a water or dry smoker but for those without a true smoker, a kettle-style grill or even a gas-fired grill can prepare good barbecue.

Smoking In A Gas-Fired Grill

While somewhat less work but also less effective for smoking than a charcoal grill, a gas-fired grill can be used to create barbecue.

Pre-heat the grill on high for 15 minutes using only one burner of the grill (assuming you have a two- or three-burner grill). Take a large handful of drained wood chips and package them securely in heavy-duty aluminum foil. Poke several holes in the foil to allow smoke to escape. Remove the grill grate from the pre-heated side of the grill and place the wood chip package on top of the lava rocks or grill plate but not directly on the gas burner.

Sam's Smoker Pro tray in a propane-fired grill

Close the lid and lower the temperature control to its lowest setting. Once smoke begins to come from the grill, open the lid, place the meat on the side of the grill away from the heat, and cook until desired internal temperature is reached. Replace the wood chip packet with new packet of drained chips every hour or so.

Smoking In A Kettle Grill

Smoking is easy to do in a kettle-style grill using indirect heat and adding wood chips to banked coals.

At least an hour before you plan to start cooking, soak wood chips or chunks in water. You'll use two chunks of wood or a good handful of wood chips for each hour of smoke-cooking. If you have any soaked wood remaining, it can be dried and used another time.

Build the fire about 40 minutes before you plan to start cooking: Remove the cooking grate from the covered grill and build a pile of about 25 to 30 charcoal pieces on one side of the fire grate; light them and let them burn down to a hot radiance, covered with gray ash. Leave only one of the bottom air vents open, directly under the charcoal. Place an aluminum loaf pan filled two-thirds full of water on the coal grate opposite from the charcoal.

Spread the hot coals with a pair of long-handled tongs to make a bed for the wood chips or chunks; place a good handful of drained chips or two chunks of wood directly on the hot coals. Replace the cooking grate on the grill and place the meat over the pan of water, on the opposite side of the grill from the fire source. Cover the grill with the top vents fully open and directly over the meat.

Maintain a temperature of about 200° F. to 225° F. If the temperature rises above 225° F., shut the bottom dampers to almost closed, monitor the heat, and open that vent again as the temperature drops.

When smoke-cooking food that takes more than an hour, you will need to add more charcoal to the fire to maintain the temperature. Start a second supply of charcoal burning in a small grill or charcoal chimney about 30 to 40 minutes after you have started cooking. This will give a steady supply of hot coals. For a very long smoke-cooking period (six to eight hours), you'll need to add eight additional briquettes to the grill every 45 minutes or so.

Throughout the smoke-cooking process watch for smoke escaping from the top vents. When it slows down or stops, add more wood chunks or chips to the fire. When adding extra wood or charcoal to the fire, work quickly with long-handled tongs: each time you take the lid off the grill, it will add 10 to 15 minutes extra cooking time.

Using A Vertical Smoker

For those reluctant to invest a lot of money in an offset smoker, vertical – or bullet – smokers are an inexpensive alternative. Although they don't have the capacity of an offset or horizontal smoker, they can be used for small briskets, Boston butts, and poultry.

Vertical smokers fueled by gas, electricity, charcoal, or wood and are generally available for under $200, depending on the fuel source. Also known as water smokers, they have a water pan set above the heat source that helps to regulate the smoker's temperature and provide moisture for the cooking food. Above the water bowl are usually two or sometimes three racks for smoking.

Wood chips, chunks, discs, or pellets are placed in a flame tray above the heat source and below the water bowl to produce smoke. If the smoker is a charcoal smoker, hardwood chunks can be used instead of charcoal to provide both heat and smoke.

One of the more popular charcoal-fired smokers is the Weber Smokey Mountain that has two 18½-inch cooking grates and a water pan. One of the better methods to get the smoker ready for a four- to six-hour low temperature smoking session is to start one or two chimney starters full of charcoal (depending on how long you plan on cooking) and when the coals are ash-covered dump them into the charcoal pan and add a handful of pre-soaked wood chips.

Fill the water pan three-fourths full of cool water and put the smoker together. The water pan will help regulate the temperature to between 225° F. and 240° F. Close the bottom air vents and leave the top vent open. Allow the smoker to come up to temperature and add whatever you're cooking. Use a remote-reading thermometer to monitor the actual temperature on the cooking grates. If the temperature drops too much, open the bottom vents slightly. Add more wood chips every couple of hours to keep a good smoke going throughout the barbecue.

Using An Offset Smoker

Offset smokers are for true barbecue enthusiasts and make creating barbecue easier than other cooking units. The offset or horizontal pit smoker has two separates sections: a cooking area and a firebox which may be fueled by split wood logs, chunks, or even charcoal with wood added for flavoring.

The benefits of offset smokers are that the cooking chamber doesn't need to be opened when refueling or adding more wood and the large cooking area that allows a whole pig or several Boston butts or briskets to be cooked at the same time. Some offset smokers also have a cover and grate over the firebox so it may be used for grilling or keeping mops and sauces warm during the barbecue.

The temperature of the smoker is regulated by the amount of fuel and dampers on the firebox. Once the temperature stabilizes around 210° F. to 230° F., add the meat placing it in the center of the cooking chamber. Baste the meat occasionally and monitor the temperature in the cooking chamber adding more charcoal or wood as needed.

Rubs, Herbs, & Spices

Rubs are dry ingredients (herbs, spices, and seasonings) that are rubbed into or sprinkled on meat before cooking to enhance the flavor and sometimes serve as a tenderizing agent. A rub has an advantage over a marinade in that it forms a crust on food when cooked. Rubs are also used to provide concentrated flavor to larger cuts of meat like beef brisket and pork shoulder where marinating is not always effective.

Ingredients in dry rubs vary depending on the kind of food and the region, but some items are more common than others are. Salt and sugar are used more often than anything else is and, not surprisingly, are also the most controversial. Some backyard cooks believe that salt draws the moisture out of meat and most agree that sugar burns on the surface of food. If making your own rubs, it's best to moderate these two ingredients. Garlic powder, onion powder, chili powder, cayenne pepper, and lemon pepper seasonings are also very popular. Secondary seasonings such as dry mustard, cumin, sage, thyme, allspice, cinnamon, nutmeg, and ginger are also commonly used.

When making your own rubs, use finer-ground spices for rubs on thinner cuts of meat as they break down and flavor the food faster. Use coarser-ground spices for larger, thicker cuts of meat as these will not break down as fast and will give you more flavors when cooking over a longer period. Keep a record of what you use so you can replicate it – or not – the next time.

Many barbecue "experts" suggest the proper ratio for rubs is eight parts brown sugar, three parts kosher salt, one part chile powder, and one part a combination of other spices such as black pepper, cayenne pepper, Old Bay® seasoning, thyme, onion powder, and garlic powder. But most backyard chefs develop their own favorite mix for different meats.

When applying a rub, do it thoroughly and evenly. Allow the flavors of the rub to penetrate the food by covering it with food film or aluminum foil and refrigerating it. Fish fillets and shrimp usually only need to marinate for 30 to 45 minutes while large cuts of meat can marinate overnight or several days.

Rub Tips

- Sprinkle the rub onto the food creating an even layer. Use a plastic cheese shaker, like those found in pizza parlors for crushed red pepper flakes and grated cheese, to distribute the rub evenly.

- Apply rubs thoroughly and evenly especially on the side of the meat.

- Don't reuse remaining rub after it has been in contact with meat. Bacteria on the meat could contaminate the rub.

- Keep salt and sugar in check when creating your own rubs.

- Use finely ground rubs on thinner cuts of meat and a coarser grind on the larger, thicker cuts.

- After applying a rub, allow the food to absorb the flavor of the rub by covering it and leaving it in the refrigerator.

- Rubs only last a few weeks before losing their intensity and flavor. It's best to mix rubs right before using.

- Turbinado sugar is a better choice for rubs as it has a higher burn temperature than regular sugar. Turbinado sugar, sold as "Sugar in the Raw," is a coarsely granulated raw cane sugar.

In the following rub and spice recipes, unless otherwise directed, simply mix the dry ingredients together. Stored in a covered container in a cool cabinet, the rubs and spice mixtures will keep for about a month.

Barbecue Beef Rub

2½ tablespoons brown sugar	2 tablespoons sweet paprika
2 teaspoons dry mustard	2 teaspoons onion powder
2 teaspoons garlic powder	1½ teaspoons dried sweet basil
1 teaspoon ground bay leaves	¾ teaspoon ground coriander
¾ teaspoon ground savory	¾ teaspoon dried thyme
¾ teaspoon cracked pepper	¾ teaspoon white pepper
¼ teaspoon ground cumin	½ teaspoon kosher salt

Cambridge Dry Rub

¼ cup dark brown sugar, firmly packed
3 tablespoons cracked pepper
2 tablespoons ground cumin
1 teaspoon garlic powder

2 tablespoons kosher salt
3 tablespoons chili powder
2 tablespoons sweet paprika
1 teaspoon lemon pepper

In the top half of a double-boiler set over simmering water, combine all the ingredients. Cook for about 20 minutes, stirring every five minutes or so, until the sugar begins to melt and mixture thickens. Remove from the heat and let the mixture cool. Pass the mixture through a sifter.

Caribbean Rub

1 tablespoon dark brown sugar
2 teaspoons onion powder
1 teaspoon kosher salt

2 teaspoons ground allspice
½ teaspoon dried thyme
½ teaspoon ground nutmeg

Mix thoroughly and use on pork.

Mason-Dixon Line Barbecue Rub

2 tablespoons kosher salt
2 tablespoons dark brown sugar
2 tablespoons chili powder
1 tablespoon ground cayenne

2 tablespoons granulated sugar
2 tablespoons ground cumin
2 tablespoons black pepper
4 tablespoons sweet paprika

All-Purpose Rub

½ cup granulated sugar
¼ cup onion salt
¼ cup seasoned salt
¼ cup sweet paprika
1 teaspoon dry mustard
¼ teaspoon dry ginger

¼ cup garlic salt
¼ cup celery salt
¼ cup black pepper
¼ cup chili powder
¼ teaspoon dried oregano
¼ teaspoon ground cloves

Kansas City Rub

2 cups granulated sugar
2 teaspoons chili powder
½ cup kosher salt
1 teaspoon garlic powder

¼ cup sweet paprika
½ teaspoon ground cayenne
2 teaspoons cracked pepper

Sirloin Rub

1 tablespoon ground cinnamon
1 tablespoon ground coriander
2 teaspoons ground cayenne

1 tablespoon sweet paprika
1 tablespoon granulated sugar
1 tablespoon kosher salt

Dry Rub for Ribs

2 tablespoons sweet paprika
2 tablespoons light brown sugar
2 tablespoons kosher salt

2 teaspoons ground cayenne
1 teaspoon dry mustard

Texas-Style Dry Rub

4 tablespoons kosher salt
1 tablespoon celery salt
2 tablespoons black pepper
2 tablespoons chili powder
1 tablespoon ground cayenne

½ tablespoon white pepper
3 tablespoons sweet paprika
½ tablespoon garlic powder
½ tablespoon dried lemon peel
1 tablespoon dry mustard

Mexican Dry Rub

2 tablespoons hot paprika
2 teaspoons ground cayenne
1 tablespoon dark brown sugar
1 teaspoon garlic powder
1 teaspoon onion powder

1 teaspoon cracked black pepper
2 teaspoons dry mustard
2 tablespoons chili powder
1 teaspoon ground cumin

Curry-Chili Rub

¼ cup chili powder
1 tablespoon curry powder
1 teaspoon dry mustard
1 teaspoon dried oregano
1 teaspoon dried parsley flakes

1 teaspoon onion powder
1 teaspoon garlic powder
1 teaspoon white pepper
2 teaspoons celery salt

Chili-Bacon Rub

2 teaspoons bacon fat, melted
½ teaspoon tomato paste
¼ teaspoon ground cayenne

1 garlic clove, crushed
2 teaspoons chili powder

Combine all ingredients in a bowl. Mash until smooth.

Beef Rub

1 teaspoon chile powder	2 teaspoons hot paprika
1 teaspoon ground cumin	1 teaspoon ground coriander
1 teaspoon kosher salt	1 teaspoon onion powder
1 teaspoon garlic powder	½ teaspoon dry mustard
½ teaspoon black pepper	½ teaspoon dried thyme
½ teaspoon curry powder	½ teaspoon ground allspice

Poultry Rub

1 tablespoon dried minced onion	1 tablespoon onion powder
2 teaspoons dried thyme	½ teaspoon kosher salt
1 teaspoon ground allspice	¼ teaspoon ground nutmeg
¼ teaspoon ground cinnamon	2 teaspoons granulated sugar
1 teaspoon black pepper	1 teaspoon ground cayenne
¼ cup snipped chives	½ cup chopped yellow onion
4 tablespoons lime juice	2 teaspoons cayenne pepper sauce

In a blender or food processor, combine all the ingredients and blend to a thick paste. (If using skinless chicken, add two tablespoons vegetable oil to the paste.) Rub the paste over the chicken, cover and refrigerate overnight.

Kansas City Rib Rub

1 tablespoon hot paprika	1 tablespoon seasoned salt
1 teaspoon black pepper	1 teaspoon ground cayenne
1 teaspoon garlic powder	1 teaspoon crushed red pepper flakes
½ teaspoon onion powder	½ teaspoon dry mustard
¼ teaspoon celery salt	¼ teaspoon chili powder
¼ teaspoon ground cumin	

Pork Rub

1½ tablespoons black pepper	1½ tablespoons brown sugar
1 tablespoon sweet paprika	½ tablespoon hot paprika
½ teaspoon ground cayenne	

Spicy San Antonio Rub

¼ cup kosher salt	¼ cup cracked black pepper
2 tablespoons garlic powder	1 tablespoon ground cumin
1 tablespoon ground cayenne	

Dry Jerk Rub

1 tablespoon dried onion flakes
2 teaspoons dried thyme
1 teaspoon ground allspice
¼ teaspoon ground cinnamon
1 teaspoon black pepper
2 teaspoons chopped chives

1 tablespoon onion powder
2 teaspoons kosher salt
¼ teaspoon ground nutmeg
2 teaspoons granulated sugar
1 teaspoon ground cayenne

Phoenix Rub

1 cup granulated sugar
¼ cup sweet paprika
½ teaspoon ground cayenne
2 teaspoons black pepper
1 teaspoon onion powder

1 cup dark brown sugar, firmly packed
2 teaspoons chili powder
½ teaspoon kosher salt
1 teaspoon garlic powder

Spicy Honey Rub

¼ cup prepared horseradish
2 teaspoons soy sauce

1 teaspoon hot paprika
2 teaspoons honey

Combine all ingredients in a bowl until smooth. Use on poultry and pork.

Galveston Rub

6 garlic cloves, crushed
2 teaspoons sweet paprika

1 teaspoon ground cayenne
1 teaspoon lemon juice

Combine all ingredients in a bowl. Mash until smooth. Use on poultry and pork.

Mustard Rub

¼ cup Dijon-style mustard
¼ cup finely chopped fresh basil
¼ teaspoon ground cayenne

2 teaspoons olive oil
½ teaspoon black pepper

Rosemary and Allspice Rub

1 garlic clove, crushed
½ teaspoon chopped rosemary

10 allspice berries, crushed
2 teaspoons olive oil

Combine all ingredients in a bowl until smooth. Use for beef, poultry, pork, and lamb.

Sesame Mustard Rub

1 garlic clove, crushed
½ teaspoon grated lime peel
2 teaspoons sesame oil

1 teaspoon mustard seeds
2 teaspoons lime juice

Mash all ingredients in a bowl until smooth. Use for beef, poultry, pork, and fish.

French Provencal Rub

4 tablespoons fresh rosemary
4 tablespoons white pepper
3 tablespoons ground allspice
2 tablespoons kosher salt

4 tablespoons fresh thyme
5 crushed bay leaves
½ teaspoon crushed juniper

West Indian Rub

3 tablespoons curry powder
2 tablespoons ground allspice
2 tablespoons ground ginger
2 tablespoons kosher salt

2 tablespoons ground cumin
3 tablespoons sweet paprika
1 tablespoon ground cayenne
2 tablespoons black pepper

Latin American Rub

4 tablespoons ground cumin
2 tablespoons ground coriander
1 tablespoon dark brown sugar
1 tablespoon crushed red pepper flakes

4 tablespoons chili powder
1 tablespoon ground cinnamon
2 tablespoons kosher salt
2 tablespoons black pepper

Mediterranean Rub

Grated peel of 2 lemons (2 tablespoons)
¼ cup fresh rosemary leaves
¼ cup coarse black pepper

¼ cup thinly sliced garlic cloves
¼ cup chiffonade of fresh sage leaves
2 tablespoons kosher salt

Oriental Rub

4 tablespoons five-spice powder
2 tablespoons ground cloves
2 tablespoons kosher salt
2 teaspoons white pepper

4 tablespoons onion powder
2 teaspoons garlic powder
2 tablespoons granulated sugar
2 teaspoons ground coriander

Southern Barbecue Rub

½ cup light brown sugar, firmly packed
¼ cup cracked black pepper
1 teaspoon dry mustard
2 tablespoons garlic powder

2 tablespoons kosher salt
¼ cup hot Hungarian paprika
1 tablespoon onion powder
2 teaspoons ground cayenne

Rack of Rib Rub

1 tablespoon sweet paprika
1 teaspoon cracked black pepper
2 teaspoons garlic powder
1 teaspoon onion powder
¼ teaspoon celery salt
¼ teaspoon ground cumin

1 tablespoon kosher salt
1 teaspoon crushed red pepper flakes
1 teaspoon ground cayenne
½ teaspoon dry mustard
¼ teaspoon chili powder

Peppercorn Beef Rub

4 tablespoons black peppercorns
4 tablespoons pink peppercorns
4 tablespoons white peppercorns
4 tablespoons green peppercorns

2 tablespoons yellow mustard seeds
2 teaspoons coarse kosher salt
3 teaspoons garlic powder
1 teaspoon onion powder

Coarsely grind peppercorns and mustard seed, combine with remaining ingredients.

Brisket Rub

¼ cup dark brown sugar, firmly packed
¼ cup crushed black pepper
1 tablespoon dry mustard
2 tablespoons garlic powder

2 tablespoons kosher salt
¼ cup sweet paprika
1 tablespoon onion powder
2 teaspoons ground cayenne

South Texas Rub

1 garlic clove, crushed
1 teaspoon Ancho chile powder
1 teaspoon seasoned salt

1 teaspoon black pepper
¼ teaspoon ground cayenne

Combine all ingredients in a bowl until smooth.

Tennessee Dry Rub

2 teaspoons dark brown sugar
2 teaspoons sweet paprika
1½ teaspoons white pepper
1½ teaspoons kosher salt

2 teaspoons coarse black pepper
1 teaspoon chili powder
1½ teaspoons ground cayenne
1 teaspoon garlic powder

Austin Rub

3 tablespoons kosher salt
3 tablespoons hot paprika
1½ tablespoons lemon pepper

3 tablespoons black pepper
3 tablespoons granulated sugar
1 tablespoon ground cayenne

Tandoori Spice Rub

1 teaspoon ground ginger
1 teaspoon ground coriander
1 teaspoon powdered turmeric
1 teaspoon ground cayenne

1 teaspoon ground cumin
1 teaspoon hot paprika
1 teaspoon kosher salt

Baby Back Rub

1 tablespoon ground cumin
1 teaspoon kosher salt
½ teaspoon ground cayenne

1 tablespoon dried thyme
1½ teaspoons black pepper
1 teaspoon garlic powder

Chili-Chicken Rub

½ cup chili powder
2 tablespoons dark brown sugar
½ teaspoon granulated garlic

½ teaspoon black pepper
1½ teaspoons ground cayenne

Lemon Pepper Thyme Rub

6 tablespoons lemon pepper
2 tablespoons sweet paprika
1 teaspoon granulated sugar
¼ teaspoon ground coriander
¼ teaspoon ground cayenne

2 tablespoons dried thyme
2 teaspoons granulated garlic
½ teaspoon kosher salt
¼ teaspoon ground cumin

Mix all ingredients together. Apply generously to steaks or burgers for 30 minutes or up to two hours before grilling.

Abby's Wild Rib Rub

¼ cup sweet paprika
¼ cup cracked black pepper
¼ cup dark brown sugar, firmly packed
1 tablespoon white pepper

1 tablespoon ground cayenne
¼ cup granulated sugar
1 tablespoon garlic powder

Rub the slab generously with prepared mustard before adding rub. Use about two tablespoons of rub for each side of a rib slab.

Southwest Seasoning

2 tablespoons chili powder
2 tablespoons hot paprika
1 tablespoon ground coriander
1 tablespoon garlic powder
1 tablespoon kosher salt

2 teaspoons ground cumin
1 teaspoon black pepper
1 teaspoon ground cayenne
1 teaspoon crushed red pepper flakes
1 tablespoon dried oregano

Meat Seasoning

½ cup kosher salt
2 tablespoons white pepper
2 tablespoons granulated onion
4 tablespoons granulated garlic

4 tablespoons black pepper
1½ teaspoons ground cayenne
1½ teaspoons ground cumin
2 tablespoons hot paprika

Seafood Seasoning

1 tablespoon ground bay leaves
1½ teaspoons dry mustard
¾ teaspoon ground nutmeg
½ teaspoon ground ginger
½ teaspoon ground cayenne
¼ teaspoon ground cardamom

2½ teaspoons celery salt
1½ teaspoons black pepper
½ teaspoon ground cloves
½ teaspoon sweet paprika
¼ teaspoon ground mace

Cajun Seasoning

2 tablespoons kosher salt
1 teaspoon lemon pepper
1 teaspoon dry mustard
½ teaspoon garlic powder

1 teaspoon black pepper
1½ teaspoons ground cayenne
1 teaspoon dark brown sugar
Pinch ground cinnamon

Cajun Spice

5 tablespoons sweet paprika
¼ cup granulated garlic
2 tablespoons dried thyme
2 tablespoons black pepper
2 tablespoons dried parsley

¼ cup coarse kosher salt
2 tablespoons dried oregano
2 tablespoons onion powder
2 tablespoons ground cayenne

This Cajun Spice seasoning is used in a number of recipes in this book. It's a good idea to have a batch on hand for whatever you're cooking!

Barbecue Spice

½ cup chili powder
3 teaspoons onion powder
1 teaspoon sweet paprika
1 teaspoon dark brown sugar
½ teaspoon dry mustard

¼ cup kosher salt
2 teaspoons ground cumin
1 teaspoon garlic powder
1 teaspoon ground cayenne
½ teaspoon grated lemon peel

Creole Seasoning

1 teaspoon kosher salt
3 teaspoons ground cayenne
2 teaspoons chili powder
2 teaspoons dried thyme

3 teaspoons black pepper
2 teaspoons garlic powder
2 teaspoons dried basil

Creole-Cajun Seasoning

2½ tablespoons sweet paprika
2 tablespoons garlic powder
1 tablespoon onion powder
1 tablespoon dried oregano
1 tablespoon dried parsley

2 tablespoons kosher salt
1 tablespoon black pepper
1 tablespoon ground cayenne
1 tablespoon dried thyme

New Orleans Seasoning

2½ tablespoons sweet paprika
2 tablespoons garlic powder
1 tablespoon onion powder
1 tablespoon dried oregano

2 tablespoons kosher salt
1 tablespoon black pepper
1 tablespoon ground cayenne
1 tablespoon dried thyme

Chipotle Paste

1 7-ounce can Chipotle chiles
3 large garlic cloves
1 teaspoon dried thyme

2 tablespoons corn oil
2 teaspoons ground coriander
1 teaspoon black pepper

Chipotle peppers in adobo sauce are available in most supermarkets. The sauce is made from ground chiles, vinegar, and herbs.

Combine all the ingredients in a food processor and process until blended but still slightly chunky, about one minute. Refrigerate the paste, tightly covered, for up to three weeks.

Jerk Paste

4 green onions, finely chopped
1 Jalapeño or Habanero pepper
1 teaspoon dried thyme
½ teaspoon ground cayenne

1 garlic clove
1 tablespoon ground allspice
½ teaspoon ground nutmeg
2 tablespoons fresh lime juice

Combine all ingredients in blender, pulse to puree mixture. Store paste in covered glass container in refrigerator. To use, rub two teaspoons or more seasoning over surface of meat. Marinate at least an hour, refrigerated, before cooking.

Jerk Seasoning For Pork

1 teaspoon celery seed
2 teaspoons ground allspice
1 teaspoon dried thyme
1 teaspoon kosher salt
1 teaspoon black pepper
½ teaspoon ground cayenne

2 teaspoons granulated garlic
2 teaspoons granulated sugar
½ teaspoon ground cinnamon
½ teaspoon ground nutmeg
2 teaspoons onion powder

Chili Powder

4 Ancho chiles
4 teaspoons cumin seed
1 teaspoon ground coriander
½ teaspoon ground cloves

3 Chipotle chiles
1 teaspoon garlic powder
1 teaspoon dried oregano

Grind together in spice grinder.

Chinese Five-Spice Powder

1 tablespoon Schezuan pepper
1 star anise
12 whole cloves

2 teaspoons fennel seed
4 1-inch long sticks cinnamon

Put ingredients in a spice grinder and grind to fine powder.

Firehall Chili Powder

6 tablespoons sweet paprika
1 tablespoon Ancho powder
1 teaspoon dried oregano
½ teaspoon garlic powder
¼ teaspoon ground cloves

1 tablespoon turmeric
1 teaspoon ground cumin
½ teaspoon ground cayenne
½ teaspoon kosher salt

Seasoned Salt

2 teaspoons black pepper
1 teaspoon onion salt
1 teaspoon garlic salt
1 teaspoon ground cumin
1 teaspoon dried parsley
½ teaspoon curry powder

1 teaspoon chicken bouillon
1 teaspoon onion powder
1 teaspoon chili powder
1 teaspoon dried marjoram
1 teaspoon sweet paprika
¼ cup kosher salt

New Mexico Spice

2 tablespoons chili powder
2 tablespoons sweet paprika
1 tablespoon ground coriander
1 tablespoon granulated garlic
1 tablespoon kosher salt

2 teaspoons ground cumin
1 tablespoon dried oregano
1 teaspoon ground cayenne
1 teaspoon crushed red pepper flakes
1 teaspoon black pepper

Dry rubbed and smoked pork tenderloin

Barbecue duck, sugar snaps, and smoked new potatoes (recipe page 109)

Grilled mahi-mahi, roasted Red Bliss potatoes, and broccoli (recipe page 169)

Sauces, Mops, & Marinades

Marinades

There are as many barbecue sauces, mops, and marinades as there are backyard grill masters and each chef has his or her favorite concoction developed to bring out the best barbecue taste, texture, and flavor.

Marinades are a highly seasoned liquid used to add a layer of flavor, tenderize meat and seafood, and add moisture before cooking.

There are three basic components of a marinade: acidic liquid, oil, and seasonings. The acid breaks down the surface tissue of the food and the seasonings add flavor while the oil adds moisture. Acids can be of various forms such as vinegar, citrus juice, tomatoes, and wine. The acid in a marinade also adds flavor. Marinade spices are usually very strong since they grow weaker during the marinating process.

Because most marinades contain acidic liquids, use non-reactive containers for marinating. Reactive materials such as aluminum may discolor and give food an unpleasant flavor. Use glass, ceramic dishes, or food-safe plastic bags.

If the marinade will also be used as a table or mop sauce, it must be boiled for at least five minutes after being used as a marinade. The boiling will destroy any harmful bacteria that could cause a foodborne illness.

- A tenderizing marinade must contain an acidic ingredient such as lemon juice, wine, or vinegar to break down the protein. Because the marinade only touches the food's surface, not much tenderization actually takes place in the tissue.

- Allow ½-cup marinade for each pound of meat or seafood.

- Marinate in a food-safe plastic bag or glass dish.

- If you use a vacuum sealer such as the FoodSaver by Tilia to marinate meats, decrease marinating time by one-half.

- Marinate at least six hours to tenderize beef. Turn or stir the meat occasionally to allow even exposure to the marinade. For flavoring only, marinate 30 minutes or up to two hours.

- Not all marinades lend themselves for use as a mop or table sauce as sometimes the flavors are too strong.

- Marinating times will vary depending on the food. Three things to remember are:

49

- If you marinate too long, the surface protein will break down completely and the food will become mushy.

- Marinades do not penetrate more than ½-inch into food and longer marinating times on larger cuts of meat will not give deeper penetration but will make the outside ½-inch of the food taste more of the marinade.

- If you marinate at room temperature the marinade will penetrate the food faster. But refrigerate any food marinating for more than an hour. Never marinate poultry at room temperature.

Marinating Times For Meat and Seafood

Food	Time (hours)	Food	Time (hours)
Beef Steaks	4 - 6	Chicken Breasts	2 - 4
Beef Kabobs	4 - 6	Chicken Pieces	3 - 4
Beef Roast	5 - 7	Chicken Wings	4 - 4
Beef Brisket	5 - 7	Whole Chicken (split)	4
Beef Short Ribs	6 - 8	Turkey	4 - 12
Pork Tenderloins	3 - 4	Turkey Quarters	4 - 8
Pork Chops	3 - 4	Duck	6 - 8
Spare Ribs	6 - 8	Game Birds	4 - 6
Lamb Kabobs	4 - 6	Fish	1 - 2
Venison	6 - 8	Shrimp	½ - 1

Mops and Bastes

The words mop and baste are interchangeable. And just to add some confusion, "mop" is also the name for the utensil used to apply a mop... a smaller version of a kitchen string mop! The liquid version of a mop is a thin liquid that usually contain acid, spices, seasonings, and sometimes oil applied to food while it is cooking to help the food retain moisture and to add another dimension of flavor.

A mop can be something as simple as beer, fruit juice, or meat stock or it can be very complex. In some cases, a marinade can become the mop after being reheated to kill any bacteria. Acidic liquids such as lemon juice, Worcestershire sauce, wine, and vinegar are common. When cooking food that tends to dry out quickly such as fish, chicken, or vegetables oil is often added to the mop.

Most mops are cooked first to blend their flavors. Keep mops warm if used right away or re-heat them if they have been refrigerated. Don't apply a cold mop to warm food.

Keep mops simmering between mopping throughout the 'Q for three reasons:

- First, you are not applying a cold liquid to warm food and extending its cooking time.

- Second, mopping food in the early stages of cooking can contaminate the mop with bacteria from the food and simmering will kill the bacteria.

- Third, the simmering process reduces the mop and concentrates its flavor.

If the meat has had a rub applied before cooking, start applying the mop after the food has cooked for half of the estimated cooking time. This allows the rub to form a crust on the meat before the mop is applied. Mop small pieces every 30 minutes and big cuts every hour or so.

A mop is daubed on these pork ribs after three hours of smoking

Sauces

Texas White Sauce

½ cup unsalted butter
⅔ cup all-purpose flour
Pinch garlic salt

½ teaspoon ground black pepper
1 (8-ounce) can evaporated milk
1 cup chicken stock

This sauce is traditionally served with chicken fried steak.

Heat butter until hot, stirring constantly, and add enough flour to form a thick roux. Add garlic salt and pepper. Lightly brown roux, lower heat and add evaporated milk and stock, stirring constantly. If necessary, thin with additional stock.

Texas Brown Sauce

½ cup meat dripping or butter
⅔ cup all-purpose flour
3 to 4 cups beef stock
Beef roast pan drippings

1 teaspoon cayenne pepper sauce
1 teaspoon Worcestershire sauce
1 teaspoon black pepper
¼ teaspoon kosher salt

Make a roux using meat drippings or butter and flour. Cook until medium brown. Add beef stock, pan drippings (if any), and seasonings. Cook and stir until gravy thickens.

Creole Sauce

2 medium onions, chopped
1 yellow bell pepper, chopped
1 stalk celery, chopped
4 cloves garlic, minced

2 tablespoons olive oil
8 plum tomatoes, chopped
1 cup chicken stock
1 teaspoon dried thyme

In a heavy saucepan heat oil and cook onions, bell pepper, celery, and garlic over medium heat until softened. Add tomatoes, stock, and thyme. Simmer about 20 minutes until most of the liquid has evaporated.

Home-Style Habanero Hot Sauce

15 Habanero chiles	1 mango, peeled and mashed
1 cup prepared mustard	¼ cup light brown sugar, firmly packed
¼ cup white vinegar	1 tablespoon curry powder
1 tablespoon ground cumin	1 tablespoon Ancho powder
½ teaspoon kosher salt	½ teaspoon black pepper

Curry powder quickly loses its pungency and should be stored no longer than two months.

Wearing food-safe gloves chop and seed peppers. Blend with remaining ingredients in food processor until smooth. Strain and refrigerate. Use cautiously: this is a sauce with a real authority, equal in intensity to the hottest commercial Habanero sauces.

Horseradish Cream Sauce

2 tablespoons mayonnaise	1½ tablespoons horseradish
¼ teaspoon cayenne pepper sauce	¼ teaspoon granulated sugar
½ teaspoon Dijon-style mustard	¼ teaspoon white vinegar
Pinch kosher salt	Pinch sweet paprika

Combine ingredients in a glass bowl. Refrigerate at least one hour before serving.

Buffalo Sauce

½ cup fresh lemon juice	¼ cup clover honey
¼ cup peanut oil	2 tablespoons grated ginger
½ cup cayenne pepper sauce	2 cloves garlic, minced

Combine ingredients in a glass bowl. Use to marinate "Buffalo" chicken wings or chicken tenders six hours before cooking.

Hot Pepper Sauce

3 cups distilled white vinegar	2 teaspoons kosher salt
2 pounds Jalapeño peppers	

Wearing food-safe gloves seed and chop peppers. Simmer vinegar, salt, and peppers over medium heat for 10 minutes. (Be careful not to breathe the fumes!) Process in a blender or food processor until smooth. Store in a glass bottle and age at least three months. Strain before use.

Habanero Pepper Sauce

12 Habanero peppers
1 tablespoon vegetable oil
½ cup chopped onion
2 cloves garlic, minced

½ cup chopped carrots
¼ cup fresh lime juice
½ cup white vinegar

Wearing food-safe gloves chop and seed peppers. Heat the oil in a medium saucepan and cook the onion and garlic until soft; add the carrots with a small amount of water. Bring to a boil, reduce heat, and simmer until carrots are soft, about 10 minutes. Place the mixture and chiles into a blender and purée until smooth. Return to stove, combine the purée with lime juice and vinegar, and simmer five minutes or until reduced by one-third.

Citrus Honey Sauce

½ cup soy sauce
¼ cup lemon juice
2 teaspoons grated lemon peel
½ teaspoon ground ginger
¼ cup honey

¼ cup chicken stock
¼ cup orange juice
1 teaspoon grated orange peel
1 clove garlic, pressed

Combine all ingredients in medium saucepan. Bring to simmer and cook until mixture has thickened and reduced by one-third.

Honey Cranberry Sauce

½ cup orange juice
2 tablespoons clover honey

½ cup whole cranberries
¼ teaspoon ground ginger

Combine all ingredients in medium saucepan. Bring to simmer and cook until cranberries have burst and mixture reduces by one-third.

Creole Mustard Sauce

1 cup mayonnaise
1 tablespoon prepared mustard
½ teaspoon cider vinegar
1 teaspoon red wine vinegar
½ teaspoon ground cayenne
1 tablespoon minced garlic
1 teaspoon celery seed

¼ cup Creole mustard
1 tablespoon horseradish
Dash Worcestershire sauce
1 teaspoon water
½ teaspoon kosher salt
1 teaspoon green bell pepper
1 teaspoon dried minced onion

Combine all ingredients in medium bowl. Mix well. Cover and refrigerate until serving.

Asian Grill Sauce for Chicken, Beef, or Pork

2 tablespoons dark brown sugar
1 cup ketchup
1 large garlic clove, minced
2 tablespoons red wine vinegar

1 teaspoon Chinese hot mustard
1 tablespoon soy sauce
2 teaspoons Asian chili paste

Combine all ingredients except chili paste in a small saucepan. Bring to a boil and then turn off heat. Stir in chili paste.

Jamaican Jerk Sauce

6 green onions, thinly sliced
2 cloves garlic, minced
2 large shallots, finely chopped
1 teaspoon minced fresh ginger
1 Habanero pepper, minced
1 teaspoon cracked black pepper
1 teaspoon ground cinnamon
1 teaspoon ground allspice
¼ teaspoon ground cayenne

½ teaspoon ground nutmeg
1 teaspoon fresh thyme
1 teaspoon dark brown sugar
1 teaspoon kosher salt
½ cup orange juice
½ cup rice wine vinegar
¼ cup red wine vinegar
¼ cup soy sauce
¼ cup olive oil

Combine green onions, garlic, shallots, ginger, and Habanero. Set aside. In another bowl, combine spices, thyme, sugar, and salt. Whisk the orange juice, both vinegars, and soy sauce into the spices. Slowly drizzle in oil while whisking constantly. Add the green onion mixture and stir. Let rest an hour before using to marinate meat or poultry.

Fiery-Hot Jamaican Jerk Sauce

1 teaspoon ground allspice
1 teaspoon kosher salt
1 teaspoon granulated sugar
1½ teaspoons black pepper
1 teaspoon ground ginger
¾ teaspoon ground cinnamon
1 teaspoon dried thyme
1 teaspoon garlic powder
1½ teaspoons ground cayenne
1½ teaspoons dried sage

¾ teaspoon ground nutmeg
2 tablespoons lime juice
¾ cup white vinegar
½ cup orange juice
¼ cup soy sauce
¼ cup olive oil
2 Habanero peppers, minced
1 cup chopped yellow onion
3 green onions, finely chopped
4 cloves garlic, minced

Mix dry ingredients. Add liquid ingredients and mix with whisk. Add peppers, onions, and minced garlic. Reserve enough marinade for basting. Use on chicken or pork.

Teriyaki Marinade and Sauce

1 cup reduced sodium soy sauce
2 tablespoons white vinegar
1 teaspoon dry mustard
½ teaspoon garlic powder
1 cup water

2 tablespoons brown sugar
½ teaspoon ground ginger
1 teaspoon ground cayenne pepper
2 tablespoons cornstarch
1 tablespoon water

Whisk together all the ingredients, except the cornstarch and one tablespoon of water. To make sauce: make slurry of the cornstarch and one tablespoon of water and whisk into the marinade. Bring to a boil, reduce heat, and stir as the sauce thickens.

Chinese Barbecue Sauce

½ cup dry sherry
4 cloves garlic, crushed
6 tablespoons soy sauce
2 teaspoons plum sauce
2 teaspoons black bean paste
6 tablespoons Hoisin sauce

2 teaspoons kosher salt
1½ teaspoons five-spice powder
½ cup granulated sugar
1 tablespoon cornstarch
1 tablespoon water

Mix well. Heat in double boiler, add cornstarch and water slurry for thickening, if necessary.

Chipotle Sauce

¼ cup cane syrup
¼ cup black coffee
¼ cup ketchup
¼ cup cider vinegar
¼ cup Worcestershire sauce

2 tablespoons chili powder
1 tablespoon corn oil
2 teaspoons prepared mustard
½ teaspoon kosher salt
6 Chipotle peppers, chopped

Mix ingredients and bring to a boil in a medium saucepan. Reduce heat and simmer 10 minutes. Transfer to blender and blend thoroughly.

Spicy Basting Sauce

1 cup orange juice
¼ cup soy sauce
1 teaspoon curry powder
½ teaspoon ground ginger

½ cup lemon juice
¼ cup dark brown sugar, firmly packed
1 teaspoon cracked black pepper
¼ teaspoon mace

Curry powder quickly loses its pungency and should be stored no longer than two months.

Combine all ingredients thoroughly. Use to baste poultry during last 30 minutes of cooking.

Rib eye Steak Sauce

4 cups ketchup

2 cups water

1 cup Worcestershire sauce

4 teaspoons seasoned salt

1 teaspoon garlic powder

1 teaspoon Bellycheer® Jalapeño
  Pepper Sauce

2 tablespoons onion powder

1 cup cider vinegar

1 tablespoon chili powder

2 teaspoons black pepper

1 teaspoon ground cayenne

1 cup dark brown sugar, firmly packed

Mix all ingredients except brown sugar. Simmer for 30 minutes. Add brown sugar, stir until smooth.

Grilled top sirloin resting before carving

Mops

Brisket Beer Mop

1 (12-ounce) can beer
¼ cup water
1 medium yellow onion, finely chopped
1 tablespoon Worcestershire sauce
1 teaspoon kosher salt
½ cup cider vinegar
¼ cup canola oil
3 cloves garlic, minced
1 teaspoon black pepper
1 teaspoon ground cayenne pepper

Mix all ingredients together in a saucepan over low heat. Cook until thoroughly dissolved. Mop over brisket every hour.

North Carolina Vinegar Mop

2 cups cider vinegar
2 tablespoons dark brown sugar
2 teaspoons crushed red pepper flakes
3 tablespoons ketchup
1 tablespoon kosher salt
2 teaspoons black pepper

Combine all ingredients in medium mixing bowl. Use to mop pork and for Carolina Slaw.

Barbecue Meat Mop

4 quarts beef stock
2 tablespoons garlic powder
3 tablespoons sweet paprika
1 quart Worcestershire sauce
2 tablespoons kosher salt
3 tablespoons dry mustard
2 tablespoons chili powder
2 tablespoons cayenne pepper sauce
2 cups cider vinegar
2 cups vegetable oil

To make beef stock, buy five pounds or more of beef bones, cover with cold water and simmer about two hours. Skim stock and add all the other ingredients to stock and let stand overnight in the refrigerator before using. Use this mop to rub over meats while cooking. Keep remaining mop refrigerated.

Pork Shoulder Mop

1 (10½-ounce) can beef bouillon
¾ cup Worcestershire sauce
¼ cup canola or vegetable oil
1 teaspoon garlic powder
1¼ cups water
½ cup cider vinegar
1 teaspoon dry mustard
1 teaspoon crushed red pepper flakes

Beef Barbecue Mop

4 cups beef stock
2 bay leaves
1 teaspoon dried oregano
2 tablespoons unsalted butter
¼ cup chopped yellow onion
¼ cup chopped celery
¼ cup chopped bell pepper
¼ cup minced garlic
2 tablespoons BBQ Beef Rub (Page 36)
½ teaspoon dry mustard
½ teaspoon kosher salt

½ teaspoon white pepper
½ teaspoon black pepper
¼ teaspoon ground cayenne
2 tablespoons grated lemon peel
5 tablespoons lemon juice
2 tablespoons soy sauce
2 tablespoons white vinegar
1 tablespoon olive oil
1 tablespoon sesame oil
1 pound finely chopped bacon

In a medium stockpot, bring stock, bay leaves, and oregano to a boil. Reduce heat to a simmer.

In a medium sauté pan, melt the butter over medium-high heat, add the onion, celery, bell pepper, garlic, beef rub, mustard, salt, white and black pepper, and cayenne. Cook until browned, about five to seven minutes. Add to broth along with the lemon peel, juice, soy sauce, vinegar, and the oils. Stir to combine.

Cook the bacon in a nonstick skillet until soft. Drain bacon and add to the broth mixture. Continue simmering until reduced by one-third, about 45 minutes to an hour. Cool and process in blender or food processor until smooth.

Caribbean Mop

1 cup chicken or beef broth
½ cup cider vinegar
2 tablespoons canola or corn oil

1 cup water
¼ cup dark rum

Soppin' Sauce

1 cup water
1½ tablespoons chili powder
½ cup ketchup
3 tablespoons Worcestershire sauce
¼ cup fresh lemon juice
½ teaspoon ground cayenne
⅓ cup dark brown sugar, firmly packed

1 (6-ounce) can tomato paste
1½ teaspoons black pepper
½ teaspoon garlic powder
¼ cup cider vinegar
½ cup unsalted butter
⅓ cup clover honey
½ teaspoon kosher salt

Combine all ingredients in a medium saucepan. Bring to boil, reduce heat, and simmer one hour, stirring occasionally. If using as a basting sauce, mop meat during cooking. This sauce also makes an excellent table sauce.

Dipping Sauces

Peppercorn Dipping Sauce

3 tablespoons soy sauce
1 tablespoon Asian sesame oil
1 tablespoon green onion
2 teaspoons Chinese chili paste
1 teaspoon minced garlic

3 tablespoons water
1 tablespoon rice vinegar
2 teaspoons granulated sugar
1 teaspoon minced ginger
1 teaspoon crushed Tellicherry peppercorns

Sweet-and-Sour Dipping Sauce

¾ cup rice vinegar
¼ cup granulated sugar
2 tablespoons dry sherry
2 cloves garlic, pressed

½ cup water
¼ cup light brown sugar, firmly packed
2 tablespoons fresh lime juice
1 teaspoon Chinese chili paste

Vietnamese Chili Sauce

2 dried red Thai chiles
2 cloves garlic
½ teaspoon granulated sugar

1 tablespoon rice vinegar
2 tablespoons fish sauce
1 tablespoon lemon juice

This is a basic hot and sour chile dipping sauce.

Finely mince chiles and garlic and place in a mortar. Mash with pestle. Add rice vinegar and sugar. Stir until sugar dissolves. Add fish sauce and lemon juice, stirring between each addition.

Variations: Use green Serrano chiles instead of dried Thai chiles; use lime juice instead of lemon juice; or use palm sugar instead of granulated sugar. (Palm sugar is from palm trees and is a common ingredient in Thai dishes.)

Mustard Dipping Sauce

2 teaspoons soy sauce
2 teaspoons Sake or Mirin

1 teaspoon Dijon-style mustard
¼ teaspoon cayenne pepper sauce

Combine all ingredients and whisk to blend well. Serve as a dip for meatballs or egg rolls.

Honey Mustard Sauce

¼ cup dry mustard
½ cup dark brown sugar, firmly packed
¼ cup vegetable oil

½ cup honey
¼ cup cider or red wine vinegar
Dash Worcestershire sauce

Combine all ingredients in a small bowl and whisk until smooth. Put into a small non-metal container and refrigerate overnight. Stir before serving.

Marinades

Cuban-Style Marinade

½ cup olive oil
8 cloves garlic, chopped
¼ cup orange juice
¼ cup fresh lime juice
¼ cup chopped fresh mint

1 teaspoon ground cumin
½ teaspoon black pepper
1½ teaspoons kosher salt
½ teaspoon dried oregano

Heat the olive oil over medium heat in a medium saucepan. Add garlic and cook until golden. Add orange and lime juices. Simmer briefly. Add remaining ingredients. Cool and use to marinate pork chops or tenderloins.

Teriyaki Marinade

1 cup teriyaki sauce (Page 56)
½ cup light brown sugar, firmly packed
1 teaspoon garlic powder
½ cup Italian salad dressing

¾ cup pineapple juice
½ cup white vinegar
¼ cup Worcestershire sauce

Spicy Beer Marinade

1 cup beer
1 teaspoon chopped fresh thyme
1 tablespoon Worcestershire sauce
3 bay leaves, crushed
½ cup chopped fresh parsley

1 cup beef stock
3 tomatoes, seeded & chopped
2 teaspoons cayenne pepper sauce
1 teaspoon black pepper
1 tablespoon lemon juice

Pork Herb Marinade

1 cup beer
¼ cup honey mustard
½ medium yellow onion, finely chopped
2 teaspoons dried rosemary
½ teaspoon black pepper

¼ cup Dijon-style mustard
¼ cup olive oil
3 cloves garlic, pressed
½ teaspoon kosher salt

Combine all ingredients; marinate pork in refrigerator at least four hours. Reserve marinade, boil and use as mop during barbecuing. (A good mustard for this is Uncle Dave's® Kickin' Horseradish Mustard.)

Beef Marinade

1 cup canola oil
½ cup lemon juice
¼ cup Dijon-style mustard
2 cloves garlic, minced

¾ cup reduced sodium soy sauce
¼ cup Worcestershire sauce
2 teaspoons black pepper

Blend all ingredients in a blender. Use to marinate two to three pounds of beef in refrigerator 24 hours before cooking.

Steak Marinade

⅔ cup pineapple juice
¼ cup cider vinegar
½ cup mild barbecue sauce
1½ teaspoons clover honey

¼ cup dark brown sugar, firmly packed
¼ cup reduced sodium soy sauce
1 teaspoon ground ginger

Combine all ingredients. Add with meat in a large shallow dish or a large re-sealable food-safe bag. Refrigerate overnight.

Fajita Marinade

¼ cup vegetable oil
1 teaspoon granulated sugar
1 teaspoon Ancho chile powder
½ teaspoon kosher salt
¼ cup fresh chopped cilantro

¼ cup red wine vinegar
1 teaspoon dried oregano
½ teaspoon garlic powder
½ teaspoon black pepper

Maple Whiskey Marinade

1 cup pure maple syrup
½ cup tarragon wine vinegar
1 tablespoon grated orange peel
3 tablespoons Dijon-style mustard

¾ cup straight Rye whiskey
½ cup orange juice
2 tablespoons dark brown sugar
½ cup teriyaki sauce (Page 56)

Brisket Marinade

½ cup white vinegar
1 (12-ounce) can beer
1 yellow onion, chopped
1 tablespoon dark brown sugar
1 teaspoon black pepper

¼ cup canola oil
1 tablespoons Colgin Liquid Smoke®
1 teaspoon kosher salt
1 teaspoon ground cayenne pepper

Chicken Marinade

½ cup soy sauce
¼ cup red wine vinegar
½ teaspoon dried basil
¼ teaspoon black pepper

¼ cup vegetable oil
1 teaspoon dried oregano
½ teaspoon garlic powder
1 teaspoon dried parsley

Combine all ingredients. Pour over chicken pieces in a non-metal dish. Cover and refrigerate overnight, turning pieces occasionally. Discard marinade after use.

Asian Marinade

1 cup orange juice
½ cup lime juice
6 green onions, sliced thin
1 teaspoon crushed red pepper flakes

½ cup lemon juice
6 tablespoons Sake or Mirin
2 small Jalapeños, sliced
1 tablespoon grated orange peel

Mix ingredients in a bowl and use to marinate seafood, chicken, or pork.

Rib 'n' Beer Marinade

1 quart beer
2 cups dark brown sugar, firmly packed
1 cup cider vinegar
1 teaspoon ground cumin

2 teaspoons crushed red pepper flakes
1 tablespoon chili powder
1 teaspoon dry mustard

Combine beer, sugar, vinegar, and spices in a large saucepan. Bring to a boil, remove from heat, and cool. This marinade goes well with any smoked or grilled meat.

BBQ Meat Marinade

1½ cups olive oil
¼ cup Worcestershire sauce
2 teaspoons kosher salt
½ cup red wine vinegar
1½ teaspoons dried parsley
2 tablespoons minced onion

¾ cup reduced sodium soy sauce
2 tablespoons dry mustard
1 tablespoon black pepper
¼ cup lemon juice
2 cloves minced garlic
1 teaspoon dried tarragon

Caribbean Pork Marinade

1 cup orange juice
½ cup fresh lime juice
1½ teaspoons ground cumin
1½ teaspoons cayenne pepper sauce
¾ teaspoon ground allspice

4 cloves garlic, pressed
1 medium yellow onion, finely chopped
1½ teaspoons granulated sugar
½ teaspoon kosher salt
½ teaspoon black pepper

Combine all ingredients. Marinate pork for four hours or overnight, refrigerated.

Jerk Marinade

1 yellow onion, chopped
6 green onions, finely chopped
1 teaspoon kosher salt
4 teaspoons ground allspice
1 teaspoon ground nutmeg
1 teaspoon ground cinnamon
6 Habanero peppers, finely chopped
1 teaspoon cracked black pepper
2 tablespoons dried thyme

4 cloves garlic, chopped
2 tablespoons ground ginger
2 tablespoons fresh lime juice
¼ cup olive oil
½ cup red wine vinegar
4 tablespoons soy sauce
4 tablespoons dark rum
2 tablespoons dark brown sugar

Mix all ingredients. Use to marinate pork or chicken.

Smoked Red Bliss potatoes with a mustard glaze

Barbecue Sauces

There are as many varieties of barbecue sauces as there are barbecue enthusiasts and backyard chefs but sauces are generally grouped into four basic categories: Eastern, Texas, Midwest, and Florida-style. Each has its own distinct flavor, taste, and purpose.

Barbecues east of the Mississippi traditionally use vinegar-based sauces while Texans prefer sauces with chili powder, Worcestershire sauce, and ground cayenne pepper. In the Midwest where Kansas City reigns as the barbecue capital, sauces use ketchup and brown sugar as a base. In some parts of the Carolinas and Florida, the choice is a mustard-based sauce.

Kansas City-style sauces – sweet and spicy – lend themselves to most barbecues: pork, beef, ribs, or chicken, while Texas-style sauces are better on brisket, ribs, and the like. Eastern sauces complement pork from tenderloins and roasts to whole hogs.

Mastering The BBQ has scores of barbecue sauces designed to whet your appetite. Each sauce has a distinct flavor: some spicier than others, some sweeter, some mild, and some come close to being outrageously hot. Experiment with them. Try them, modify them, and create your own. Each barbecue pitmaster and backyard chef has a signature sauce… use these recipes as a springboard to develop your own signature sauce!

Barbecue sauces are a combination of ingredients: sweet, sour, and spicy added to a base such as ketchup- and tomato-based sauce for a red sauce, prepared mustard for a mustard sauce, cider vinegar for a vinegar sauce, and other ingredients such as tomato purée, chopped tomatoes, chili sauce, and chicken or beef stock. Some, including many restaurants, even use commercial sauces as a base before adding their own ingredients for a unique taste.

A variety of tastes and textures combine in a good barbecue sauce. There's sweetness, a little sour bite, some heat, and, to give a good mouth-feel, usually some fat such as butter or oil.

Sauces are a subject of serious disagreement both amongst backyard chefs and competition barbecue teams. Some argue that the sauce makes the barbecue and if you don't serve a sauce, it is not barbecue. Others will say if the food needs a sauce, it doesn't qualify as barbecue. Even those who agree that sauce is good for barbecue disagree which style sauce is best.

Regardless of the never-ending sauce debate, sauces are becoming an important barbecue component. In almost every barbecue competition, you can now find a barbecue sauce category. Use barbecue sauces as a condiment, a dipping sauce, a glaze, or a combination of all three. Sauces should balance, not overwhelm, the flavor of the barbecue.

When you are ready to begin creating your own sauce, look for a balance of sweet, sour, and spicy flavors, in that order. Like doing a 'Q, getting the perfect sauce combination is more an art than a science.

The following table gives some of the more common liquids, herbs, spices, and seasonings used for sauces:

Sweet	Sour	Seasonings	Heat
Cane syrup	Balsamic vinegar	Capers	Ancho chiles
Corn syrup	Cider vinegar	Dry mustard	Black pepper
Dark brown sugar	Lemon juice	Kosher salt	Bellycheer®
Granulated sugar	Lime juice	Marjoram	Jalapeño Sauce
Hoisin Sauce	Pick-A-Peppa®	Old Bay®	Cayenne pepper
Honey	Red wine vinegar	Oregano	Chipotle chiles
Jellies	White vinegar	Parsley	Curry powder
Maple syrup	Worcestershire	Soy sauce	Garlic
Molasses	sauce		Ginger
Tennessee			Habanero chiles
Gourmet™ Sauce			Horseradish
			Jalapeño chiles

Aromatics	Mouth-feel	Liquids	Mustard
Bell pepper	Bacon fat	Beer	Onions
Carrots	Beef stock	Bourbon	Pickled Jalapeños
Celery	Butter	Coffee	Red pepper flakes
Garlic	Chicken stock	Red Wine	Tabasco® sauce
Onions	Lard	Soda/Cola	Tennessee
Spices	Vegetable Oil	Stocks	Gourmet™ Sauce
Steak sauce		Water	Texas Pete® sauce
Sun-dried			Wasabi
tomatoes			White pepper

Tennessee Gourmet™ Apple & Spice Flavors

One of the commercial products featured in a number of *Mastering The BBQ* recipes is the Tennessee Gourmet™ line of gourmet sauces. The Apple & Spice sauce is a unique blend of flavors that can be used for marinating, glazing, basting, and as a dipping sauce. It is available in four flavors:

"Sensible" – a slightly sweet, flavor rich sauce with no heat.

"Sneaky Hot" – includes Habanero chiles. Called "sneaky" because the initial sensation doesn't appear to be too hot… but watch out!

"Silly Hot" – more Habaneros so it may bring a tear to your eye!

"Stupid Hot" – not a sauce for the faint of heart or palate, but for the experienced chile head!

Sauces By Region

Region	Characteristics
Alabama	Thin – Vinegar-base with sugar, salt, pepper, and mayonnaise
Georgia	Thin – Mustard-based, tomato, and vinegar
Kansas City	Thick – Tomato and sugar base, sweet, smoky, and spicy
Kentucky	Black sauce with Worcestershire sauce, molasses, and vinegar
Florida	Tomato-based, lemon, lime, vinegar, and butter
Hawaiian	Sweet and sour, with fruits and fruit juices
Oriental	Soy sauce, peanuts with some heat
N. Carolina (Eastern)	Thin – Vinegar-based with crushed red peppers, salt, and pepper
N. Carolina (Western)	Thin – Similar to Eastern but with tomato and sugar added
South Carolina	Thin – Mustard, vinegar, salt, and pepper
Tennessee	Depends on the region. Thin, vinegar-tomato sauce or sweet, somewhat spicy tomato-based with peppers and molasses (Memphis)
Texas	Very thick – Tomato-based, spicy with molasses and Worcestershire sauce; also a thin, hot-pepper based sauce

Sauce Tips

- Only apply sauces with sugar in the final stages of cooking or they will burn. Granulated sugar will begin to burn at 265° F.

- A barbecue sauce should complement the food not overpower it.

- When making a sauce, use fresh ingredients whenever possible.

- When you make a new sauce, write down what you do so that you can repeat it – or not.

- Don't be afraid to experiment with different ingredients when making barbecue sauces.

- If you have tomatoes in the sauce, be careful not to burn them while cooking the sauce; burned tomatoes will create a bitter taste.

- Just like slow-cooking meat, cooking sauce with low heat over time is better than cooking quickly with high heat.

- As the sauce ages, the taste will change. The day after you make a sauce, it may taste great, but then two weeks later it may taste bland.

- Always refrigerate sauce when storing it.

Many agree that an ideal barbecue sauce should taste *sweet*, then *sour*, and finally *hot*. In the true sense of barbecue, sauces are only added during the last few moments of cooking or not added at all and served on the side.

Great barbecue is a continuing quest to find the correct combination of temperature, rubs, mops, wood chips, and sauces to make the perfect barbecue! And, just when you believe your 'Q can't be any better, along comes another idea, another recipe, another suggestion, and the quest begins anew! Enjoy the journey.

Basic Barbecue Sauce

1 stick (½ cup) unsalted butter
1 yellow onion, chopped
4 cloves garlic, chopped
2 Jalapeños, chopped
2 tablespoons hot paprika
2 cups ketchup
1½ tablespoons Old Bay®
¼ cup dark molasses

4 tablespoons Worcestershire sauce
½ teaspoon black pepper
6 tablespoons lemon juice
1 teaspoon kosher salt
1 whole tomato, finely chopped
1 12-ounce can beer
¼ cup dark brown sugar, firmly packed

This is a basic barbecue sauce for pork or beef to use as a base for your own creations!

Melt butter in large saucepan over medium heat. Add onion, garlic, and Jalapeños, cook until onions sweat. Add paprika and cook briefly. Add remaining ingredients; simmer at low heat for an hour.

Kansas City Sauce

2 cups ketchup
2 tablespoons cayenne pepper sauce
1 green bell pepper, chopped
¼ cup fresh lemon juice
¼ cup Dijon-style mustard
¼ cup Worcestershire sauce

1½ cups dark brown sugar, firmly packed
1 yellow onion, chopped
5 cloves garlic, minced
1 teaspoon sweet paprika
2 tablespoons cider vinegar

Combine all ingredients in a saucepan. Bring to a boil. Reduce heat and simmer for 30 minutes, stirring occasionally. Cool sauce and purée in food processor or blender.

Arkansas BBQ Sauce

3 cups water
½ cup Worcestershire sauce
1 cup ketchup
1 tablespoon crushed red pepper flakes
1 cup dry white wine

½ cup dark brown sugar, firmly packed
½ cup Dijon-style mustard
1 tablespoon black pepper
1 quart red wine vinegar
¼ cup kosher salt

In a medium saucepan, combine ingredients and bring to boil. Reduce heat and simmer for about 30 minutes.

Pig Pickin' Sauce

½ cup (1 stick) unsalted butter
3 ribs celery, chopped
3 large cloves garlic, chopped
1 medium onion, chopped
1 cup chili sauce
½ cup dark brown sugar, firmly packed
2 bay leaves
1 cup beef stock

1 teaspoon ground cayenne
1 teaspoon ground cumin
1 teaspoon Ancho chile powder
½ teaspoon black pepper
½ cup cider vinegar
¼ cup Worcestershire sauce
¼ teaspoon kosher salt
¼ cup Jack Daniel's® sour mash

Divide butter into eight pieces. In a medium saucepan over moderate heat, melt two tablespoons butter. Add celery and cook one minute. Add garlic and onion; cook until onions sweat. Add butter, one tablespoon at a time; cook until melted. Add remaining ingredients, except whiskey, and simmer for 30 minutes, stirring occasionally.

Add whiskey and continue to simmer for five minutes. Allow sauce to cool. Remove bay leaves and blend sauce in blender or food processor until smooth. Return to heat and bring to simmer. Serve over pork or serve as table sauce. (This makes about four cups of sauce that has authority!)

Abby's Rib Sauce

¾ cup light brown sugar, firmly packed
1½ tablespoons chili powder
2 teaspoons dry mustard
1 teaspoon ground ginger
½ teaspoon ground allspice
½ teaspoon ground cayenne

¼ teaspoon ground nutmeg
¼ teaspoon black pepper
1 cup white vinegar
¼ cup dark molasses
¼ cup water
4 cups ketchup

In a large saucepan, combine the brown sugar, chili powder, mustard, ginger, allspice, cayenne, nutmeg, and black pepper. Add the vinegar, molasses, and water. Stir until dry ingredients dissolve. Add the ketchup and stir to mix. Bring to a boil over medium heat, stirring constantly. Reduce the heat to low, cover, and simmer for 30 minutes. Remove from the heat and let cool to room temperature.

Danielle's BBQ Sauce

2 tablespoons olive oil
1 yellow onion, chopped
1 head garlic, minced
½ cup dark brown sugar, firmly packed
1 tablespoon cayenne pepper sauce

1 tablespoon Colgin Liquid Smoke®
1½ cups ketchup
3 tablespoons Jack Daniel's® Sour Mash
½ teaspoon dry mustard

Heat oil in a medium saucepan over medium heat and cook the onion and garlic until tender. Add the remaining ingredients. Bring to a boil. Reduce heat and simmer for 30 minutes.

Champion Barbecue Sauce

4 cups tomato sauce
1½ cups Dr Pepper or cola
1½ cups cider vinegar
1½ cups chili sauce
¼ cup prepared mustard
½ cup bottled steak sauce
6 tablespoons lemon juice
½ cup Worcestershire sauce

2 tablespoons vegetable oil
1 tablespoon soy sauce
3 teaspoons cayenne pepper sauce
1¼ cups dark brown sugar, firmly packed
2 tablespoons black pepper
2 tablespoons garlic salt
1 tablespoon dry mustard

In a large saucepan, combine the tomato sauce, Dr Pepper, vinegar, chili sauce, mustard, steak sauce, lemon juice, Worcestershire sauce, oil, soy sauce, and cayenne pepper sauce. Stir well. Bring to a simmer over medium heat.

In a small bowl, combine the brown sugar, pepper, garlic salt, and dry mustard. Stir to blend. Add the dry ingredients to the tomato mixture and stir well.

Increase the heat to medium-high and bring to a brisk simmer, stirring frequently. Cook uncovered for about 20 minutes. Cover the saucepan and reduce the heat to low. Cook for about 30 minutes until the flavors are well blended. Cool to room temperature. Use immediately or cover and refrigerate up to one week.

Tennessee Barbecue Sauce

1 yellow onion, chopped
1 tablespoon unsalted butter
1 cup tomato sauce
½ teaspoon Bellycheer® Jalapeño
  Pepper Sauce

1½ teaspoons kosher salt
¼ cup Worcestershire sauce
1 cup cider vinegar
¼ cup water

In a medium saucepan over medium heat, cook onion in butter until soft. Combine remaining ingredients and bring to boil. Reduce heat and simmer for 30 minutes, stirring occasionally.

Finger-Lickin' Sauce

1 tablespoon olive oil
1 tablespoon unsalted butter
1 yellow onion, chopped
1½ tablespoons Worcestershire sauce
2 cups ketchup
1 teaspoon celery seed
2 tablespoons Tamari soy sauce
6 tablespoons lemon juice
½ teaspoon garlic powder

1 tablespoon A-1® sauce
1½ teaspoons Tabasco® sauce
¾ cup dark brown sugar, firmly packed
½ teaspoon ground sage
1 cup beer
½ teaspoon black pepper
1 teaspoon kosher salt
2 tablespoons beet horseradish

Cook onion in butter and oil over medium heat until slightly caramelized. Add remaining ingredients, except horseradish. Bring mixture to boil, reduce heat and simmer, uncovered, for 15 minutes, stirring occasionally. Cool and process or blend until smooth. Add horseradish and serve.

Not Your Traditional BBQ Sauce

2 tablespoons unsalted butter
1 yellow onion, chopped
2 cloves garlic, minced
½ cup chopped celery
¼ cup chopped bell pepper
¼ cup cider vinegar
1 teaspoon celery seed
3 tablespoons dark molasses
½ teaspoon ground allspice

2 teaspoons dry mustard
1 6-ounce can tomato paste
1 14½-ounce can tomatoes
½ teaspoon ground clove
1 teaspoon lemon juice
1 bay leaf
1½ teaspoons kosher salt
4 teaspoons Tabasco® sauce
1 lemon, quartered

In a medium saucepan over medium heat, cook onion and garlic in butter until softened. Add celery and bell pepper, cook briefly. Add remaining ingredients; bring to boil. Reduce heat and simmer, uncovered, 30 minutes, stirring occasionally. Remove bay leaf and lemon sections. Process or blend until smooth.

Secret Sauce

1 large yellow onion, minced
1 head garlic, minced
2 green bell peppers, chopped
3 tablespoons olive oil
1 cup dark brown sugar, firmly packed
½ cup A-1® Bold steak sauce

6 cups ketchup
2 cups pure maple syrup
6 tablespoons cayenne pepper sauce
6 tablespoons cider vinegar
1 cup Worcestershire sauce
½ cup water

Cook onion, garlic, and peppers in oil until tender. Add remaining ingredients. Bring to boil, reduce heat, and simmer 20 minutes.

Molasses Orange Barbecue Sauce

1 (10¾-ounce) can tomato soup
½ cup light molasses
½ cup dark brown sugar, firmly packed
1 tablespoon dried onion
1 tablespoon dry mustard
1 tablespoon grated orange peel
½ teaspoon black pepper

1 (8-ounce) can tomato sauce
½ cup white vinegar
¼ cup vegetable oil
1 tablespoon seasoned salt
1 tablespoon Worcestershire sauce
1½ teaspoons sweet paprika
¼ teaspoon garlic powder

Combine all ingredients in a medium saucepan. Bring to a boil; reduce heat and simmer, uncovered, for 20 minutes. Use to baste beef or poultry during last 15 minutes of grilling.

Down Under Barbecue Sauce

1½ cups tomato purée
1 teaspoon kosher salt
¼ cup cider vinegar
½ teaspoon black pepper

⅓ cup Worcestershire sauce
1 can beer *
1 teaspoon sweet paprika

The beer used for this recipe is Guinness Stout, however if a light meat such as pork or chicken is on the menu, use a lighter beer. For lamb, use rosemary instead of paprika.

Combine all ingredients and heat to simmer. Brush over meat every five minutes as the meat cooks. (This is not a sweet sauce.)

Hickory Barbecue Sauce

¼ cup Worcestershire sauce
4 tablespoons dark brown sugar
1 stick butter
4 cups ketchup
2 cloves garlic, crushed
1 cup hickory barbecue sauce

4 tablespoons Tabasco® sauce
¼ cup lemon juice
1 tablespoon prepared mustard
1 medium yellow onion, grated
1 teaspoon BBQ Beef Rub (Page 36)

Combine all ingredients in a medium saucepan and bring to a low boil. Reduce heat and cook for about 30 to 45 minutes until thick. Stir occasionally.

Honey Barbecue Sauce

¾ cup chopped yellow onion
1 clove garlic, chopped
¼ cup olive oil
1 cup ketchup
½ cup Worcestershire sauce
1½ teaspoons kosher salt

1 teaspoon cracked black pepper
1 cup clover honey
1 cup red wine vinegar
1 tablespoon dry mustard
1 teaspoon dried oregano
½ teaspoon dried thyme

In a medium saucepan over medium heat, cook onion and garlic in oil until tender. Add remaining ingredients and bring to a boil, stirring constantly. Reduce heat and simmer for five minutes.

Wrangler Barbecue Sauce

¼ cup dark brown sugar, firmly packed
2 teaspoons kosher salt
1 cup cider vinegar
2 cups water
1 teaspoon Tabasco® sauce

¼ cup vegetable oil
1 teaspoon granulated garlic
¾ cup lemon juice
½ cup Worcestershire sauce

Combine all ingredients in saucepan. Bring quickly to boil. Reduce heat and simmer 10 minutes.

Grand Canyon Barbecue Sauce

1 stick unsalted butter
1 onion, finely chopped
1 clove garlic, chopped
1 cup chili sauce
2 tablespoons brown sugar
½ tablespoon mustard

1 (12-ounce) can beer
3 tablespoons white vinegar
1 cup water
2 tablespoons Worcestershire sauce
2 tablespoons lemon juice
½ teaspoon ground black pepper

In a medium saucepan over medium-high heat, melt butter and cook onion and garlic. When the onion is translucent, add the remaining ingredients. Bring to a boil. Reduce heat and simmer for 15 minutes.

Cattle Ranch Barbecue Sauce

½ cup white vinegar
½ pound unsalted butter
1 tablespoon ground cayenne
1 cup Worcestershire sauce
1 tablespoon kosher salt
1 teaspoon garlic salt

½ cup bacon fat, melted
1 tablespoon black pepper
2 yellow onions, chopped
3 cups ketchup
1 tablespoon celery salt

Combine all ingredients in a medium saucepan and simmer on very low heat for at least 30 minutes. This is an excellent sauce for Spare ribs and makes enough for 10 pounds of meat.

"Swiss Chalet" Style Barbecue Sauce

3 cups water
1 cup chicken stock
¼ cup tomato juice
1½ teaspoons sweet paprika
1 teaspoon granulated sugar
¾ teaspoon kosher salt
¼ teaspoon dried basil
¼ teaspoon dried parsley
¼ teaspoon poultry seasoning
¼ teaspoon dried thyme

¼ teaspoon ground ginger
¼ teaspoon dry mustard
¼ teaspoon onion powder
1 bay leaf
¾ teaspoon Worcestershire sauce
¼ teaspoon Tabasco® sauce
2 teaspoons lemon juice
1 tablespoon cornstarch
1 tablespoon water
1 tablespoon vegetable oil

"Swiss Chalet" is a Canadian restaurant chain.

Pour water, chicken stock, and tomato juice into a medium saucepan. Add paprika, sugar, salt, basil, parsley, poultry seasoning, thyme, ginger, mustard, onion powder, bay leaf, Worcestershire sauce, and Tabasco®. Whisk to mix. Bring to a boil, then reduce heat and simmer five minutes. Remove bay leaf. Stir in lemon juice. Mix cornstarch and one tablespoon of water. Add to mixture and cook, stirring constantly, about two minutes until sauce thickens. Whisk in oil. Brush this sauce on chicken during cooking and serve at the table as a dipping sauce.

Missouri Barbecue Sauce

2 tablespoons vegetable oil
2 cloves garlic, minced
1 tablespoon chili powder
1 teaspoon sweet paprika

¾ cup cider vinegar
½ teaspoon granulated sugar
1 teaspoon dry mustard
½ teaspoon ground cumin

Combine all ingredients in a small saucepan, heat to boil. Remove from heat and allow to cool at least an hour for flavors to blend.

Texas-Style Barbecue Sauce

½ pound pickling spices
1 teaspoon whole cloves
1 medium onion, chopped
2 cups ketchup
1 quart water
1 tablespoon dry mustard
½ cup light brown sugar, firmly packed
1 tablespoon kosher salt

2 tablespoons lemon juice
2 stalks celery, chopped
2 cups chili sauce
½ cup cider vinegar
½ cup Worcestershire sauce
¼ tablespoon garlic powder
1 tablespoon Bellycheer®
  Jalapeño Pepper Sauce

Cut an eight-inch cheesecloth square and form into a bag. Add pickling spices and cloves; tie securely. Combine all ingredients in a medium saucepan; bring to a boil. Reduce heat and simmer, uncovered, about 1½ hours. Remove from heat and cool. Remove spice bag. Process in two-cup batches until sauce is smooth.

Spicy Texas Sauce

1½ cups finely chopped yellow onion
1 tablespoon unsalted butter
1 teaspoon vegetable oil
2 Jalapeños, seeded and finely chopped
2 cloves garlic, chopped
1 12-ounce can beer

1 cup ketchup
¼ cup fresh lime juice
½ cup dark brown sugar, firmly packed
2 teaspoons crushed red pepper flakes
1 tablespoon Worcestershire sauce
12 ounces tomato paste

In a medium saucepan, cook onions in butter and oil until soft; add Jalapeños and garlic, cook briefly. Add remaining ingredients and bring to a low simmer. Simmer for 30 minutes.

Apple Barbecue Sauce

1 cup ketchup
¼ cup cider vinegar
¾ teaspoon garlic powder
½ cup Tennessee Gourmet™
  Sneaky Hot Apple & Spice Sauce

¼ cup apple cider
¼ cup reduced sodium soy sauce
¾ teaspoon white pepper
¼ cup grated yellow onion
1 tablespoon green bell pepper

Combine ingredients in a medium saucepan and bring to a boil. Reduce heat and simmer 15 minutes.

Tangy Sweet Barbecue Sauce

3 large sweet onions, chopped
6 tablespoons unsalted butter
3 cups ketchup
1 teaspoon ground cayenne
½ cup lemon juice
3 teaspoons chili powder
½ teaspoon Tabasco® sauce

6 tablespoons cider vinegar
1 tablespoon Worcestershire sauce
½ teaspoon kosher salt
2 tablespoons prepared mustard
1½ cups water
6 tablespoons dark brown sugar

In a medium saucepan over medium heat, cook onion in butter until barely caramelized. Add remaining ingredients and simmer for 30 minutes.

Chef's Barbecue Sauce

2½ cups chopped yellow onions
1 cup vegetable oil
1½ cups dark brown sugar, firmly packed
3 teaspoons kosher salt
5 cups ketchup

3 cups water
1½ tablespoons mustard
1½ tablespoons Worcestershire sauce
½ cup cider vinegar

In a medium saucepan over medium heat, cook the onions in oil without allowing them to brown. Add remaining ingredients. Simmer for 30 minutes to thicken.

Citrus Barbecue Sauce

1 yellow onion, chopped
¼ teaspoon ground cayenne pepper
1 tablespoon Chipotle powder
1 Ancho chile, chopped
2 tablespoons vegetable oil
1 tablespoon chopped cilantro

½ cup fresh lime juice
2 tablespoons fresh lemon juice
1 teaspoon kosher salt
1 cup orange juice
2 tablespoons granulated sugar

Cook onion, ground cayenne pepper, Chipotle powder, and Ancho chile in oil, stirring frequently until onion is tender, about five minutes. Stir in remaining ingredients. Heat to boiling and reduce heat to low. Simmer, uncovered, about 10 minutes, stirring occasionally.

Colleen's Supreme Sauce

1 stick unsalted butter
1 yellow onion, chopped
4 cloves garlic, chopped
4 tablespoons Worcestershire sauce
6 tablespoons lemon juice
½ teaspoon black pepper
1 teaspoon kosher salt
2 tablespoons hot Hungarian paprika

1 (8-ounce) can tomato sauce
2 cups ketchup
1½ tablespoons Old Bay® seasoning
¼ cup cane syrup
1 whole tomato, finely chopped
1 (12-ounce) can beer
½ cup dark brown sugar, firmly packed

Melt butter in large heavy pot over medium heat. Add onion, garlic, Worcestershire sauce, lemon juice, pepper, salt, and paprika. Cook until onion is soft. Stir in remaining ingredients. Simmer at low heat, uncovered, for an hour.

Austin-Style Spicy Barbecue Sauce

1 cup ketchup
½ cup dark brown sugar, firmly packed
¼ cup fresh lime juice
2 tablespoons Ancho powder
1 tablespoon corn oil
1 tablespoon Worcestershire sauce

1½ cups chopped yellow onion
2 Jalapeño chiles, finely chopped
2 cloves garlic, finely chopped
12 ounces tomato paste
1 (12-ounce) can beer

In a medium saucepan, heat all ingredients to a boil. Reduce heat to low. Cover and simmer one hour, stirring occasionally.

Chicken Barbecue Sauce

2 tablespoons unsalted butter
2 tablespoons finely chopped onion
1 tablespoon green bell pepper
1 cup water
1 cup ketchup

1 teaspoon kosher salt
1 teaspoon celery seed
2 tablespoons dark brown sugar
2 teaspoons fresh lemon juice
2 teaspoons dry mustard

Plain and simple, this sauce is a good all-around sauce for chicken and a good springboard to create your own poultry sauce.

In a medium saucepan over medium high heat, cook onion and peppers in butter until tender. Add remaining ingredients. Bring to low boil, reduce heat, and simmer 20 to 30 minutes.

Tropical Barbecue Sauce

1 cup water
1 cup dark brown sugar, firmly packed
3 tablespoons ketchup
1 tablespoon soy sauce

1 cup crushed pineapple, drained
1 teaspoon dry mustard
1 tablespoon cornstarch
2 tablespoons water

In a medium saucepan, mix together one cup of water and brown sugar. Add ketchup, soy sauce, pineapple, and mustard. Bring to boil, reduce heat, and simmer 10 minutes. Dissolve cornstarch in two tablespoons of water; add to sauce and cook until sauce thickens.

Deep South Barbecue Sauce

1 cup cider vinegar
1 tablespoon grated fresh ginger
2 tablespoons dry mustard
1¼ cups ketchup
5 tablespoons Worcestershire sauce
1 clove garlic, minced

1 cup light brown sugar, firmly packed
1 lemon, thinly sliced
3 tablespoons unsalted butter
½ teaspoon kosher salt
2 tablespoons lemon juice

Combine the vinegar, grated ginger, mustard, ketchup, Worcestershire sauce, garlic, brown sugar, and lemon slices in a saucepan. Bring to a boil, reduce heat, and simmer 15 minutes. Add the butter and simmer two minutes longer. Stir in the salt and lemon juice. Strain before using.

Walter Jetton's Barbecue Sauce

3 cups ketchup
½ cup dark brown sugar, firmly packed
½ cup water
1 green bell pepper, finely chopped
2 tablespoons white vinegar

1 cup honey
½ cup Worcestershire sauce
1 medium yellow onion, finely chopped
2 tablespoons Tabasco® sauce
2 teaspoons garlic powder

This sauce is attributed to President Johnson's pitmaster.

Mix all ingredients together in a medium saucepan. Bring to a boil over medium heat. Reduce heat and simmer until onion and pepper are tender.

Simple Rib Sauce

3 tablespoons olive oil
4 cloves garlic, minced
¼ cup dark brown sugar, firmly packed
½ cup chicken stock
3 tablespoons Dijon-style mustard

1 tablespoon crushed red pepper flakes
¼ cup cider vinegar
¼ cup ketchup
2 tablespoons soy sauce

Heat the oil in a small, heavy saucepan over medium heat. Add garlic and cook until softened, two to three minutes. Do not allow the garlic to burn. Whisk in remaining ingredients, reduce heat to low; simmer 15 to 20 minutes until the mixture thickens. Stir occasionally.

Texas Table Sauce

¾ cup cider vinegar
¾ cup warm water
1 tablespoon kosher salt
1 teaspoon black pepper
1 teaspoon hot Hungarian paprika
2 tablespoons dark brown sugar
1 tablespoon dark molasses

3 tablespoons dry mustard
½ cup ketchup
3 tablespoons Worcestershire sauce
2 tablespoons dried onion flakes
¼ cup chili sauce
1 clove garlic, minced
1 cup unsalted butter

In a medium saucepan, combine vinegar and water. Stir in salt, pepper, paprika, brown sugar, molasses, and dry mustard. Bring to boil over medium low heat. Stir in remaining ingredients and simmer, uncovered, for an hour.

Beef Rib Table Sauce

3 large yellow onions, finely chopped
2 tablespoons unsalted butter
1 clove garlic, chopped
1 cup ketchup
1 cup tomato sauce
1 cup water
1 tablespoon Ancho powder
½ teaspoon ground cloves

½ cup dark brown sugar, firmly packed
1 cup beef stock
1 teaspoon Colgin Liquid Smoke®
2 teaspoons granulated sugar
3 tablespoons lemon juice
1 teaspoon black pepper
1 cup cider vinegar

In a medium saucepan over medium heat, melt butter and cook onions until soft. Add garlic and cook briefly. Add remaining ingredients and simmer over low heat for 30 minutes to an hour or until sauce reduces by one-third.

Tennessee Rib Sauce

½ cup ketchup

¼ cup dark molasses

1 tablespoon light brown sugar

½ cup orange juice

1 teaspoon grated orange peel

¼ cup Tennessee Bourbon

1 medium yellow onion, finely chopped

1 clove garlic, finely chopped

1 teaspoon dry mustard

1 teaspoon Worcestershire sauce

½ teaspoon crushed red pepper flakes

Mix ingredients in medium saucepan and bring to a low simmer over medium heat. Simmer for 30 minutes.

Kentucky Black Sauce

1 cup Kentucky Bourbon

6 tablespoons soy sauce

4 cloves garlic, crushed

1 teaspoon black pepper

1 cup canola oil

4 tablespoons Worcestershire sauce

½ teaspoon kosher salt

Mix ingredients in medium saucepan and bring to a low boil over medium heat. Remove from heat and cool.

Kentucky Barbecue Sauce

¼ cup chopped yellow onion

2 tablespoons unsalted butter

2½ cups water

1 teaspoon dry mustard

½ teaspoon cayenne pepper sauce

1 clove garlic, crushed

2 tablespoons Worcestershire sauce

1 tablespoon granulated sugar

2½ teaspoons black pepper

¼ cup cider vinegar

1 teaspoon kosher salt

2 teaspoons chili powder

In a medium saucepan over medium heat melt butter and cook onions until soft. Add remaining ingredients and bring to a low simmer. Simmer for 10 minutes.

Ellen's Rib Glaze

1 head garlic
1 tablespoon olive oil
1 tablespoon water
½ cup water
1 cup pineapple juice
¼ cup teriyaki sauce (Page 56)

3 tablespoons lemon juice
1 tablespoon soy sauce
1¼ cups dark brown sugar, firmly packed
1 tablespoon Bourbon whiskey
¼ teaspoon cayenne pepper
1 tablespoon crushed pineapple

Cut top off garlic head, drizzle with one tablespoon of olive oil and one tablespoon of water, wrap in foil. Seal package and roast in 350° F. oven for an hour. Remove garlic from oven and cool. Squeeze roasted garlic into small bowl.

Combine water, pineapple juice, teriyaki sauce, lemon juice, soy sauce, and brown sugar in a medium saucepan. Bring to a low simmer over medium heat, stirring occasionally. Add two teaspoons roasted garlic paste, Bourbon, cayenne, and crushed pineapple. Simmer for 30 minutes or until mixture reduces by one-half.

Think of barbecue as simple food? Think again!
This was one of the entries presented to judges at the
Jack Daniel's invitational barbecue competition.

Carolina Barbecue Sauces

- **North Carolina Eastern:** vinegar base, no tomato, with crushed red pepper and sugar
- **North Carolina Western (Piedmont):** vinegar base with small amounts of tomato
- **South Carolina:** mustard base usually with some tomato and molasses
- **Charlotte:** thin tomato

Unless otherwise noted, prepare the following sauces by mixing ingredients together in a non-reactive container. Sauces may be stored, covered and refrigerated, several weeks.

North Carolina Eastern Rub and Sauce

Rub

2 teaspoons granulated sugar	2 teaspoons kosher salt
2 teaspoons ground cumin	2 teaspoons dark brown sugar
2 teaspoons black pepper	2 teaspoons chili powder
¼ cup sweet paprika	1 teaspoon ground cayenne pepper

Sauce

1 cup cider vinegar	1 cup white vinegar
1 tablespoon crushed red pepper flakes	1 tablespoon granulated sugar
1 tablespoon black pepper	1 tablespoon Tabasco® sauce

North Carolina Eastern Style with Herbs

1 cup cider vinegar	1 clove garlic, crushed
¾ cup minced yellow onion	½ teaspoon kosher salt
1 teaspoon cracked black pepper	1 teaspoon granulated sugar
2 teaspoons crushed red pepper flakes	¾ teaspoon dried thyme
1 bay leaf	3 teaspoons dry mustard
3 tablespoons vegetable oil	1 teaspoon cold water
½ cup water	

Mix all ingredients except dry mustard and one teaspoon of water, in a medium saucepan; simmer five minutes. Dissolve mustard in one-teaspoon water and add to sauce.

North Carolina Piedmont-Style

1½ cups white vinegar	¾ cup ketchup
½ cup water	1 tablespoon granulated sugar
½ teaspoon crushed red pepper flakes	½ teaspoon black pepper
½ teaspoon kosher salt	

Combine ingredients in a medium saucepan and simmer over low heat until sugar dissolves.

North Carolina Western-Style

1 cup tomato sauce
¼ cup cider vinegar
2 tablespoons dark brown sugar
2 tablespoons Worcestershire sauce
½ teaspoon kosher salt
¼ teaspoon ground cayenne

¼ cup ketchup
¼ cup water
1 tablespoon sweet paprika
1 teaspoon dry mustard
¼ teaspoon chili powder

Combine ingredients in a medium saucepan and simmer for 10 minutes. Refrigerate at least 12 hours before using.

South Central Carolina Baste/Barbecue Sauce

3 tablespoons peanut oil
1 medium yellow onion, minced
¼ cup cider vinegar
2 tablespoons honey
2 tablespoons dry mustard
½ teaspoon kosher salt

2 garlic cloves, crushed
½ cup ketchup
2 tablespoons lemon juice
1 tablespoon dark brown sugar
1 teaspoon ground ginger

Mix all ingredients in saucepan. Bring to boil, reduce heat, and simmer 10 minutes.

South Central Carolina Gold Sauce

1½ cups prepared mustard
4 tablespoons tomato paste
1 tablespoon Worcestershire sauce
½ teaspoon black pepper

5 tablespoons dark brown sugar
3 tablespoons cider vinegar
½ teaspoon cayenne pepper
½ teaspoon garlic powder

Combine ingredients in a medium saucepan and simmer for about five minutes to dissolve sugar.

Eastern North Carolina-Style Barbecue Sauce

1 gallon cider vinegar
¼ cup kosher salt
2 tablespoons ground cayenne

3 tablespoons crushed red pepper flakes
½ cup dark molasses

Mix all ingredients together.

Beef

Smart Shopping

Appearance, grade, and selecting the right cut for the way the meat is being cooked are all critical considerations when choosing beef for barbecue or grilling.

Appearance

- Select beef with a bright red color without any grayish areas.
- Look for steaks that are firm to the touch.
- Make sure the package is cold and has no tears.
- Choose packages without excessive liquid.
- Purchase beef before the sell-by date and cook or freeze it promptly.

Grades

Grading, which is a voluntary program, is based on the amount of marbling (flecks of fat) and the age of the animal. It gives an indication, but not a guarantee, of tenderness, juiciness, and flavor. The higher the grade, the better the quality of the meat. The U.S. Department of Agriculture Food Safety & Inspection Service inspects beef to insure wholesomeness. Most producers and processors also have their meat graded by the federal Agricultural Marketing Service.

There are eight quality grades for beef although only the top three are usually sold at retail: Prime, Choice, and Select. The remaining grades are standard, commercial, utility, cutter, and canner.

Prime – The highest grade. Prime has the most marbling and is available in limited quantities. Prime is sold in fine restaurants and specialty meat markets. Prime meat is rarely sold in supermarkets. (Prime rib, by the way, is not necessarily Prime grade meat but rather a cut of meat.)

Choice – Choice has less marbling than Prime but more than Select. It is typically found in the butcher's meat case at the grocery store. Choice beef is wet-aged as opposed to the highest end Prime that is dry-aged although some Prime is also wet-aged.

Select – Select has uniform quality but has the least amount of marbling of the top three grades, making it leaner and possibly less tender or flavorful than Prime or Choice. Select is usually found in the self-service meat case at the grocery store.

Quality grades are excellent guides in determining the superiority of middle meats – T-bones, Rib eyes, and tenderloin. Again, the higher the grade, the better chance that the steak will be great for the grill. When it comes to end meats – chuck and round cuts – quality grading is not as important. A Select brisket will usually provide as good a piece of beef as a Choice brisket.

These are the various beef cuts commonly used for barbecue and grilling. Plan on 12 to 16 ounces of uncooked meat per person:

Porterhouse or T-Bone: comes from the short loin and has a section of filet. They are premier cuts for grilling and should be one- to 1¼ -inches thick.

Top Loin: is next to the Porterhouse and T-Bone. It should be one- to 1½-inches thick. Boneless top loin is also called Strip steak, Kansas City steak, and New York Strip steak. With the bone in, the steak is known as a Sirloin strip, County Club steak, and Delmonico steak.

Rib Steak (Rib eye): is from the first few ribs. It should be ¾- to one-inch thick. This steak is also called Delmonico or Market steak.

Sirloin Steak: often has a large amount of bone. It should be one- to 1½ -inches thick.

Top Sirloin: is a boneless cut from the end of the loin also sometimes called a London broil. However, the same name is often used for other cuts such as shoulder and top round and also represents a restaurant style of cooking more than a specific type of beef cut.

Flank Steak: comes from the back of the belly and is best broiled quickly over a hot fire and sliced on the diagonal into thin strips. Many restaurants serve this as a London broil.

Filet or Tenderloin: is sometimes cooked whole and then sliced into serving pieces or cut into individual portions and then grilled or pan-fried. Individual cuts of filet are:

- **Chateaubriand:** a thick diagonal cut.
- **Tournedos:** thick slices tied with larding around them.
- **Filet mignon:** cut from the smaller ends of the filet.

What's The Best? The best cut is a matter of individual preference but professional chefs rate steaks in the following order based on flavor and tenderness: Tenderloin (including Filet Mignon and Chateaubriand), Porterhouse, T-Bone, New York Strip, Boneless Top Sirloin, Boneless Rib eye, and Club.

Keeping The Quality

Fresh beef, obviously, is perishable and, like all perishable food, it must be stored and handled properly to avoid spoilage and foodborne illness.

Storage

Keep It Cold Buy beef just before checking out of the supermarket. If it will take longer than 30 minutes to get home, keep it cold in a cooler with some ice packs. When you get home, immediately place beef in the meat compartment or the coldest part of your refrigerator. If you purchased beef already wrapped in food film, no additional wrapping is needed. However, you may want to place it in a plastic bag to prevent possible leakage. If the beef is only wrapped in butcher's paper, re-wrap it with food film.

Freeze For Longer Storage Freeze any beef you do not plan to use within a few days. Store it at 0° F. or colder. Label each package with the date and contents.

Beef can be frozen in its original packaging for up to two weeks. For longer storage, re-wrap beef in freezer paper, plastic freezer bags, or heavy-duty aluminum foil. Vacuum packaging is also an excellent method for prolonged storage.

Rubs & Marinades For Beef

Rubs and marinades are great ways to add flavor and tenderize beef.

Rubs are a blend of herbs, peppers, spices, and seasonings used to add flavor to steaks and roasts by coating the surface of the beef with the mixture prior to cooking.

- Rubs can consist of only dry ingredients or some include oil, crushed garlic, or other liquids that cause the rub to form into a paste.

- Rubs can be applied to the surface of the beef just before grilling or roasting or applied several hours (or even days) in advance. Refrigerate rubbed meats until they are ready to be cooked.

Marinades are a highly seasoned liquid also used to add another layer of flavor and to tenderize meat.

- Marinades usually consist of fruit or vegetable juices, wine, water, or oil combined with seasonings and herbs.

- A tenderizing marinade must contain some acidic ingredient like lemon juice, yogurt, wine, or vinegar or a natural tenderizing enzyme found in fresh fruits such as papaya, ginger, and pineapple.

- Allow ½-cup marinade for each pound of beef.

- Marinate meat in the refrigerator. If meat marinates at room temperature, limit the time to less than an hour.

- Beef must marinate at least six hours to tenderize tough cuts. Turn or stir the meat occasionally to allow even exposure to the marinade. For flavoring, marinate 15 minutes or as long as four hours.

How Much Beef To Cook

The amount of edible cooked beef a pound of raw beef will yield varies with the cut. This table will help you gauge how much beef to buy for a backyard feast. Of course, other factors will also affect the amount you need including the type of occasion and individual appetites.

Beef Cut	Yield (per pound) cooked & trimmed	Three-ounce servings per pound
Steaks Lean Boneless Steaks: Top Sirloin, Boneless Top Loin, Tenderloin, Flank, Chuck Shoulder, Top Round, and Round Tip	10½ to 12 ounces	3½ to 4
Bone-In Steaks Porterhouse, T-Bone, Rib eye, and Chuck Top Blade	7½ to 9 ounces	2½ to 3
Roasts Lean Boneless Roasts: Tenderloin, Tri-Tip, Eye Round, Round Tip	12 ounces	4
Rib eye Roasts	9 to 10½ ounces	3 to 3½
Bone-in Rib Roasts	7½ ounces	2½
Pot Roasts Boneless Chuck Pot Roasts	7½ to 9 ounces	2½ to 3
Bone-In Chuck Pot Roasts	6 to 7½ ounces	2 to 2½

Beef Cut	Yield (per pound) cooked & trimmed	Three-ounce servings per pound
Round Roasts	10½ to 12 ounces	3½ to 4
Brisket	7½ to 9 ounces	2½ to 3
Ground Beef	12 ounces	4
Stir-Fry Beef	12 ounces	4
Beef Kabobs	12 ounces	4
Stew Beef	7½ to 9 ounces	2½ to 3
Short Ribs		
Bone-In	4½ to 7½ ounces	1½ to 2½
Boneless	7½ to 9 ounces	2½ to 3

Brisket

Brisket is a term used to describe a specific part of the animal – the muscle group between the front legs. So it can come from any bovine animal: cow, bull, steer, or heifer. Brisket sold at the grocery store comes from the fed cattle supply, which is from steers – castrated bulls – and heifers, a female that has not had a calf and typically is less than 2-years-old.

Use an untrimmed beef brisket for slow smoking and barbecue. During the long cooking time, the fat will render and soak the meat keeping it moist. The untrimmed fat cap will also help retain the meat's juices.

Cooking a brisket is not a quick after-work meal. Brisket requires eight to 12 hours of cooking at a stable temperature of 200° F. to 225° F. with minimal smoke exposure after the first few hours to produce good barbecue.

Brisket can be cooked in just about any type of grill or smoker. While it is easier to cook in a larger smoker with an offset firebox, a drum, kettle-style grill, vertical smoker, or any other type of barbecue contraption can also be used. An offset smoker – usually a custom-built one – is what is most-commonly used in Texas.

Choosing A Brisket

Selecting the best brisket to barbecue is a combination of knowledge, luck, and timing. Brisket comes from the lower chest of a steer or heifer below where chuck meat comes from… a naturally tough area. You will never find a tender uncooked brisket. Brisket is sold without the bone and divided into two sections: the flat cut that has minimal fat and is usually more expensive and the more flavorful point cut which has more fat.

For Texas-style barbecue brisket, use the whole brisket, containing the flat and the point, known as the packer's cut or packer trim that has a thick layer of fat. A full brisket will weigh from six to 12 pounds. The "point" is the thicker end and the "flat" is the thinner end.

Do not chose the largest brisket but instead select a cut in a six- to 10-pound range. (A brisket will lose about 50% of its weight during cooking.) Try to get a flexible brisket. Place your hand under the center of the brisket. Select one that has the most natural bend. If it is tough coming out of the butcher shop, it will be more difficult to make it tender during the barbecue.

Look for a brisket that has about ¼-inch fat cap across the top. With the brisket lying down and the fat side up, try to pick one that is equally thick all the way across the flat.

A beef brisket ready to be seasoned and smoked

Seasoning A Brisket

Marinating is not very effective when cooking a large piece of meat as thick as a brisket. The only way to make brisket tender is to cook it slowly and at a low temperature. To make it flavorful, use a dry rub for seasoning.

Remove the brisket from its packaging and soak it for about an hour in a gallon of cold water mixed with a cup of white vinegar. Rinse well and pat dry. Take a pastry brush and paint the brisket with a light coat of prepared yellow (ballpark-variety) mustard. The mustard coating accomplishes a few things... First, it helps keep the meat moist during cooking. Second, it helps to seal the meat and set up a crust with the dry rub. Third, the acidic mustard will help to tenderize the meat. Fourth, it helps keep the dry rub on the brisket.

Cover the meat thoroughly with a liberal amount of dry rub. Wrap the brisket in food film and refrigerate it overnight or up to a day.

The next day, about 12 hours before you plan to serve the brisket, get the smoker or whatever you are using for the barbecue ready. Build a bed of coals by burning down sufficient wood chunks or charwood to bring the whole grill up to 350° F. and then shut down the lower air intake to reduce the temperature to 225° F.

Cooking Brisket

A thermometer placed at the same level as the meat should read approximately 200° F to 225° F. throughout the cooking time. Since many grill and smoker thermometers are located higher than the cooking grate, temperature readings of 235° F. to 250° F. are tolerable because the actual temperature at the cooking surface will be in the desired range. A remote-reading thermometer makes monitoring the temperature easier.

Place the meat as far away from the heat source as possible. This provides for a more even cooking temperature. If it is too close to the heat source, one side will cook at higher temperatures than the other will and the brisket will not have a consistent tenderness. If you have a smaller grill (such as a Weber kettle-style grill) place the charcoal on one side of the charcoal grate and the meat on the opposite side of the cooking grate. Rotate the meat every 30 minutes (when you baste the meat) to keep the cooking temperatures even. If you are using a vertical cooker, use a pan under the meat to catch the juices to prevent flare-ups and to act as a diffuser. A water pan with about two inches of liquid is ideal and will keep the dripping juices from scorching and flavoring the meat with a burned taste. The water pan can also be partially filled with an aromatic mixture of vinegar, water, garlic, and onions.

A 10-pound brisket will usually take eight to 12 hours to smoke-cook. (A good starting point is to figure a minimum of an hour per pound uncooked weight.) Smoke the brisket over mesquite for three hours at 200° F. to 225° F., then cook another hour per pound without smoke or until the internal temperature reaches 160° F. Turn the brisket over and mop it every two hours so the bottom side doesn't get too much heat and dry out. Always check a brisket for the correct internal temperature in the thickest part of the flat not in the point.

As said before, doing a 'Q is an art, not a science. Some inexperienced backyard cooks have the idea that barbecue is like baking... follow the recipe to exact measurements, time, and temperature, and all will turn out perfectly. It doesn't often happen with traditional cooking and just won't happen when you're doing a barbecue.

When To Mop (Baste)

Do not baste the brisket when you begin cooking. Allow the rub to thicken and dry out a bit before basting (two to three hours into the barbecue). Earlier basting will only rinse off the rub and remove that layer of flavor.

After a few hours of smoking, begin basting the brisket every hour or so with a marinade to intensify the flavor.

Basting should be done with the use of a barbecue mop or a hand-held spray bottle. A barbecue mop has a 12- to 16-inch wooden handle with cotton tassels on the end... a small version of a floor mop. It is great for soaking up lots of liquid and quickly and gently dabbing the mop onto the meat. When you mop, do not rub; that removes the rub!

Serving A Cooked Brisket

Remove the brisket from the barbecue and allow it to rest about 10 minutes. Divide it into three pieces. With the lean side of the brisket up, cut off the deckle end (the point). Now turn the brisket over with the fat side up and cut off the skirt. (The grain runs in a different direction than in the flat.) With the skirt removed, trim the fat off it, top and bottom, and where it connects to the flat. Turn the skirt so that you are cutting against the grain and make the slices at about a 30- to 45-degree angle. Cut slices off the point also going against the grain and do the same to the flat. Mix the different cuts together and serve.

Basic Brisket

1 4½- to 6-pound beef brisket
1 gallon water

1 cup white vinegar
½ cup prepared (yellow) mustard

Brisket Rub

¼ cup dark brown sugar, firmly packed
¼ cup cracked black pepper
1 tablespoon dry mustard
2 tablespoons granulated garlic

2 tablespoons coarse kosher salt
¼ cup sweet paprika
1 tablespoon onion powder
2 teaspoons ground cayenne pepper

Mop

1 (12-ounce) can beer
1 cup cider vinegar
2 tablespoons brown sugar
2 teaspoons black pepper

1 cup white vinegar
2 tablespoons granulated garlic
2 teaspoons crushed red pepper flakes
1½ teaspoons kosher salt

Water/Drip pan liquid

1 quart water
½ cup cider vinegar

1 large onion, roughly chopped
1 head garlic, roughly chopped

Soak brisket in one gallon of cold water mixed with one-cup white vinegar for 20 minutes. Rinse brisket with cold water and pat dry. Brush with prepared mustard. Mix rub ingredients together in a small bowl. Liberally apply rub to brisket. Wrap in food film and refrigerate overnight. Remove from refrigerator and bring to room temperature, about an hour. Soak two cups of hickory or mesquite chips in water for an hour.

Prepare mop by mixing ingredients together in a medium saucepan. Bring to low simmer and keep warm over low heat.

Prepare smoker or grill for indirect cooking. If you are using a kettle-style grill, start 15 briquettes in charcoal chimney. When the coals are ash-covered, place them on one side of the charcoal grate. Place a disposable aluminum casserole or roasting pan on the opposite side and add the smoker liquid. Add a handful of drained chips to the briquettes. Cover grill. When a good smoke develops and the temperature stabilizes around 225° F., place the brisket on the cooking grid on the side opposite from the charcoal. Cover the grill and maintain temperature of 200° F. to 225° F. Add additional briquettes and wood chips as needed. Smoke the brisket three to four hours, turning and mopping every hour. Continue slow cooking an additional three to four hours.

After four to six hours of cooking, wrap the brisket in double sheets of heavy-duty aluminum foil, add ½ cup of the mop, tightly seal and return to grill for another two hours, keeping temperature at 225° F.

When brisket reaches 160° F. internal temperature, remove the foil and place the brisket back on the grill to finish cooking to an internal temperature of 165° F. About 30 minutes before serving paint brisket with finishing sauce, if desired.

Basic Brisket Finishing Sauce

2 tablespoons unsalted butter	1½ teaspoons Tabasco® sauce
1 cup ketchup	¼ teaspoon kosher salt
3 tablespoons Dijon-style mustard	1 teaspoon black pepper
2 tablespoons cider vinegar	¼ teaspoon ground cloves
2 tablespoons Worcestershire sauce	½ cup finely chopped sweet onion
1 tablespoon dark brown sugar	2 tablespoons granulated sugar
1 tablespoon lemon juice	¼ teaspoon ground cumin
½ tablespoon Ancho powder	

Combine ingredients in medium saucepan and bring to a low simmer over medium heat. Cook until reduced by one-third.

Dallas Brisket

1 (4- to 6-pound) trimmed brisket

Dallas Rub

2 tablespoons coarse kosher salt	2 tablespoons dark brown sugar
2 tablespoons sweet paprika	2 tablespoons chili powder
2 tablespoons black pepper	

Marinade

1 (12-ounce) can beer	2 tablespoons Dallas Rub
½ cup cider or white vinegar	1 medium onion, chopped
2 Chipotle chiles, finely chopped	¼ cup canola oil
2 tablespoons Colgin Liquid Smoke®	2 tablespoons adobo sauce

The night before cooking the brisket, stir together the dry rub ingredients in a small bowl. Combine two tablespoons of the rub with the other marinade ingredients in a blender and puree. Place the brisket in a food-safe plastic bag and pour the marinade over it. Refrigerate overnight. Before beginning barbecue, bring brisket to room temperature. Drain and discard the marinade. Rub brisket with all but two tablespoons of the remaining rub, coating it well. Let the brisket sit at room temperature for about 45 minutes. Prepare the smoker for barbecuing, bringing the temperature up to 225° F. Transfer the brisket to the smoker and cook for three hours. Place the meat on a sheet of heavy-duty foil, sprinkle it with the rest of the rub, and close the foil tightly. Cook for an additional two to three hours until well done and tender. Let the brisket sit at room temperature for 15 minutes before carving.

Barbecue Brisket of Beef

1 (4-pound) trimmed beef brisket	2 tablespoons brown sugar
1 cup dry white wine	1 tablespoon minced garlic
3 cups apple cider	1 tablespoon minced ginger
¼ cup honey	1 tablespoon whole coriander
2 tablespoons Dijon-style mustard	2 sprigs fresh thyme
¼ cup soy sauce	1 tablespoon minced garlic

Combine wine, cider, honey, mustard, soy sauce, brown sugar, garlic, ginger, coriander, and thyme in Dutch oven or heavy roasting pan. Add brisket. Cover tightly and place in oven. Heat oven to 350° F. and cook for two hours. Remove brisket from cooking liquid, cover and set aside. Transfer liquid to medium saucepan and cook over medium heat until reduced to a glaze.

Using a kettle-style grill, light 15 to 20 charcoal briquettes and add small chunks of mesquite and hickory on one side of grill. Arrange brisket on grill so it is on the opposite side of the burning coals. Paint with glaze. Cover grill and smoke brisket two to three hours, or until tender, turning meat and coating with glaze every 30 minutes. Add charcoal or wood, as needed, to keep temperature at 225° F. Remove brisket from grill, allow to rest 15 minutes before carving.

Kansas City-Style Smoked Brisket

1 (5- to 8-pound) beef brisket	¼ cup olive oil
¼ cup ground cayenne pepper	½ cup water
¼ cup cracked black pepper	½ large yellow onion, finely chopped
½ cup sweet paprika	½ cup cider vinegar
¼ cup granulated garlic	8 cloves garlic, chopped

Combine dry ingredients and set aside. Coat brisket with the olive oil and rub spices into meat. Wrap brisket with food film and refrigerate at least six hours or overnight. Remove from refrigerator and let brisket come to room temperature about an hour before cooking.

Prepare smoker or charcoal grill for indirect cooking. When the grill is ready, add soaked and drained hickory wood chunks or chips. Place a drip pan in the grill; add ½-cup water, ½-cup cider vinegar, onion, and garlic. When the heat stabilizes at 225° F., place the brisket over the drip pan and cover the grill. Smoke the brisket for four hours, keeping the temperature steady by replenishing coals and wood chips as needed. After four hours, mop brisket with drip pan juices and continue smoking for another two to three hours. After that time, mop again and wrap brisket in aluminum foil. Return to smoker and cook an additional one to two hours. Remove the brisket from the smoker and let the brisket rest for 15 minutes before slicing.

Vietnamese Grilled Steak

1 pound Top Round steak
1 pkg. thin Chinese noodles
¼ cup rice vinegar
3 tablespoons soy sauce
3 tablespoons garlic puree
3 tablespoons granulated sugar
¼ teaspoon crushed red pepper flakes

¼ teaspoon kosher salt
2 tablespoons fish sauce (Nouc Mâm)
1 tablespoon water
¾ cup bean sprouts, blanched
1 cup sliced red bell pepper
2 tablespoons chopped fresh mint

Simmer the pasta in boiling, salted water until just tender; drain, rinse in cold water, and drain well. Combine the vinegar, soy sauce, garlic, sugar, crushed red pepper flakes, salt, and fish sauce with one tablespoon of water. Pour over the noodles, add the mint, and toss to mix well. Pat steak dry with a kitchen towel, season with salt and pepper. Sear on a very hot grill for three to four minutes per side; remove to a cutting board to rest for five minutes. Bias-slice the steak across the grain into thin strips. Lay a bed of noodles onto the center of a serving platter. Arrange the bean sprouts around the noodles. Place the red bell pepper on top of the bean sprouts. Fan the steak on top of the noodles and garnish with fresh mint.

Hickory-Smoked Hamburgers

1½ pounds ground round
¼ teaspoon kosher salt
4 tablespoons minced red onion

1 teaspoon Worcestershire sauce
½ teaspoon black pepper
¼ teaspoon garlic powder

Mix all ingredients together. Form into four patties. Add hickory wood to charcoal and smoke-cook burgers for about eight to 10 minutes, turning once. Serve on a grilled bun with barbecue sauce.

Simple Pepper Steak

2 (8-ounce) Sirloin steaks
3 tablespoons cracked pepper

¼ cup Cognac, warmed
½ teaspoon kosher salt

Pat steaks dry with paper towels. Firmly press crushed peppercorns into both sides of the meat. Grill steaks over hot coals until browned on both sides. Carefully pour warm cognac over steaks and ignite. Once the flame goes out, scrape off the excess pepper, salt to taste, and serve.

Thai Beef Strips

2 pounds Top Round steak, thinly sliced

Marinade

¼ cup granulated sugar

2 tablespoons sesame seeds

¼ cup finely chopped coriander

1 tablespoon minced ginger

½ cup reduced sodium soy sauce

6 cloves garlic, chopped

¼ cup thinly sliced green onions

Dipping Sauce

¼ cup granulated sugar

2 tablespoons cornstarch

¼ cup soy sauce

3 tablespoons rice vinegar

¾ teaspoon crushed red pepper flakes

Combine marinade ingredients. Add beef strips, cover, and refrigerate at least two hours before grilling. Grill beef strips over high direct heat about one minute per side.

To make the dipping sauce, combine sugar and cornstarch in a saucepan. Add soy sauce, vinegar, and crushed red pepper flakes. Stir all ingredients over low heat. Continue stirring and increase heat slightly until mixture begins to bubble and thicken.

Fajitas Strips

1 (1½-pound) Flank or Skirt steak

1 tablespoon chili powder

2 tablespoons Pick-a-Peppa® sauce

¼ cup vegetable oil

Juice and grated peel of two limes

¼ cup dark soy sauce

1 clove garlic, minced

Slice steak into thin 1½-inch strips, sprinkle with chili powder, and place in a resealable plastic bag. Combine remaining marinade ingredients and pour over steak. Refrigerate overnight. Thread meat onto skewers and grill until medium-rare, about two to three minutes.

San Antonio Steak

2 (8-ounce) New York strip steaks
4 tablespoons unsalted butter

2 tablespoons olive oil
1 yellow onion, chopped fine
1 cup chopped roasted chiles
¼ teaspoon kosher salt

4 large mushrooms, sliced thin

Sauce

1 teaspoon minced fresh cilantro
1 teaspoon minced Jalapeño
¼ teaspoon dried oregano

About 30 to 40 minutes before cooking time, apply a steak rub and bring steaks to room temperature. Prepare the sauce: Heat the oil in a small saucepan and add the onion, cook the onions until soft. Add the remaining ingredients and cook for five minutes. Keep the sauce warm. Heat the butter in a small skillet and add the mushrooms. Cook until mushrooms are soft, about five minutes. Grill the steaks to the desired doneness, turning once. Transfer the steaks to a heated platter. Spread the mushrooms over the steaks. Cover each steak equally with the green chile sauce.

Korean Barbecue

2 pounds beef tenderloin
¼ cup dark soy sauce
3 tablespoons green onion
2 teaspoons minced ginger
1 tablespoon granulated sugar
1 tablespoon Asian sesame oil

½ cup reduced sodium soy sauce
½ cup water
3 teaspoons crushed garlic
½ teaspoon black pepper
2 tablespoons sesame seeds

Cut the beef across the grain into very thin slices, and then cut into narrow strips. In a glass or stainless steel dish, mix all remaining ingredients together. Add the beef and stir thoroughly. Cover and marinate for at least three hours. Preheat grill. Cook steak strips two to three minutes per side for medium rare.

Tequila Barbecued Beef Steaks

4 (8-ounce) strip steaks,
  cut 1- to 1½-inches thick
2 tablespoons olive oil
2 teaspoons grated lemon peel

½ cup Tequila
1 clove garlic, minced
1 tablespoon black pepper
½ teaspoon kosher salt

Put meat in a one-gallon plastic food bag. Add oil, lemon peel, Tequila, and garlic; seal bag and turn to mix seasonings. Set bag in a bowl; marinate, refrigerated, at least an hour or up to six hours; turning bag over occasionally. Drain steaks, season with salt and pepper and place on a grill four to six inches above a bed of hot coals. Turn steaks to brown evenly. For medium-rare steak, cook 12 to 14 minutes.

Dijon Steak

1 1½-inch Top Loin steak
4 teaspoons Dijon-style mustard

2 teaspoons lemon juice

Tenderize steak by pounding on both sides the edge of a chef's knife or a meat tenderizer. Combine lemon juice and mustard and spread over both sides of steak. Marinate, refrigerated, at least four hours. Bring to room temperature. Broil steak on a hot grill four to five minutes on each side.

Barbecue Flank Steak

1 (1½-pound) Flank steak
½ teaspoon kosher salt
¼ cup dark brown sugar, firmly packed
2 tablespoons olive oil
¼ cup fresh lemon juice

2 tablespoons dry mustard
¼ teaspoon black pepper
2 tablespoons soy sauce
1 garlic clove, chopped

Whisk together ingredients, except steak, in bowl to make marinade. Place tenderized Flank steak in shallow non-reactive pan. Pour marinade over steak. Cover and refrigerate for at least eight hours. Remove steak from marinade and grill five to six minutes per side. Allow to rest for five minutes and then thinly slice across the grain.

Teriyaki Steak Hors D'oeuvres

1 (1½-pound) Sirloin steak
¼ cup honey
½ cup finely chopped yellow onion
½ teaspoon grated ginger

½ cup vegetable oil
¼ cup soy sauce
1 clove garlic, minced

Cut steak across the grain into thin strips. Combine remaining ingredients in large bowl and add steak. Marinate steak, refrigerated, for several hours or overnight. Remove strips from marinade, thread onto skewers. Grill over medium heat until well browned, turn once and baste with reheated marinade.

Chili Barbecue Beef

1 (1½-pound) Flank steak

Marinade

4 teaspoons ground cumin
2 teaspoons chili powder
¼ teaspoon ground cinnamon
¼ cup olive oil
¼ cup fresh lime juice

¼ cup balsamic vinegar
2 tablespoons molasses
2 tablespoons chopped oregano
1 tablespoon minced garlic

Marinade: Combine cumin, chili powder, and cinnamon. Cook spices in a dry sauté pan over high heat about 45 seconds or until fragrant. Whisk in remaining ingredients and simmer for five minutes. Cool and pour marinade over meat in shallow dish, turning to coat. Cover and refrigerate at least four hours or overnight.

Bring meat to room temperature 30 minutes before grilling. Grill beef over medium coals, basting occasionally, seven to eight minutes per side for medium-rare. Let steak rest for five minutes and slice thinly across the grain.

Barbecue-Spiced Grilled Tenderloin Steaks

2 (6-ounce), 1-inch thick
  Tenderloin steaks
1 tablespoon sweet paprika
1 teaspoon ground allspice

1 tablespoon dark brown sugar
1 teaspoon dry mustard
½ teaspoon black pepper

Combine spice ingredients in small bowl. Rub mixture generously on both sides of the steaks. Prepare grill for direct high heat grilling. Grill steaks to desired doneness, about five minutes per side for medium-rare.

Thai Beef

1 (1½-pound) Sirloin steak
3 tablespoons soy sauce

3 tablespoons fish sauce

Dipping Sauce

1 tablespoon chopped cilantro
¼ cup fish sauce (Nouc Mâm)
5 tablespoons fresh lime juice

1 tablespoon dried Piquin chiles
1 tablespoon green onion

Make dipping sauce one day ahead, cover, and refrigerate. Freeze steak for 30 minutes to make cutting easier. Slice steak into strips diagonally across the grain, about ½-inch wide, then cut the strips into bite-size pieces. Marinate the meat in soy sauce and fish sauce for about an hour. Place the meat on a fish/kabob tray and grill, turning occasionally, until done, about two to three minutes per side.

Spicy Beef Satay

1 pound Sirloin steak,	2 cloves garlic, minced
¾- to 1-inch thick	2 tablespoons dark brown sugar
¼ cup soy sauce	1 teaspoon ground ginger
¼ cup dry sherry	1 teaspoon crushed red pepper flakes
2 tablespoons Asian sesame oil	¾ cup water
¼ cup sliced green onions	½ cup chunky peanut butter

Place steak in freezer 30 minutes to firm; slice across grain into ¼-inch thick strips. In shallow glass dish, combine soy sauce, sherry, sesame oil, onion, garlic, sugar, ginger, and ½ teaspoon of crushed red pepper flakes. Add beef strips; turn to coat with marinade. Cover and refrigerate two to four hours. Soak 24 eight-inch bamboo skewers in water for 30 minutes. Drain beef; reserve two tablespoons of the marinade. Thread beef strips, accordion-style, on skewers.

In small saucepan, combine reserved marinade, remaining ½-teaspoon crushed red pepper flakes, the water, and peanut butter. Heat over low heat eight to 10 minutes or until sauce is thick and warm (adding more water if necessary). Grill satays on uncovered grill over medium-hot coals for two minutes. Turn and cook two minutes longer. Serve beef strips with sauce.

Vietnamese Grilled Beef

1 (8-ounce) Skirt steak

Marinade

1 stalk Lemongrass, minced	1 tablespoon granulated sugar
3 tablespoons fish sauce (Nouc Mâm)	¼ cup olive oil
1 Jalapeño pepper, finely chopped	2 cloves garlic, minced
1 small yellow onion, sliced	

Whisk together all the marinade ingredients. Marinate steak, refrigerated, at least four hours. Remove from marinade and bring to room temperature. Heat marinade to boil, reduce heat, and simmer five minutes. Grill steak over high heat until medium rare, about two minutes per side. Allow steak to rest for five minutes and slice across the grain. Baste with reserved marinade.

Country Fair Barbecue Sandwiches

2½ pounds boneless beef Chuck
2½ pounds boneless Boston butt

2 tablespoons black pepper

2 (12-ounce) cans beer
2 ribs celery, cut in large pieces
2 carrots, cut in large pieces
8 whole cloves
¼ teaspoon black pepper

2 tablespoons unsalted butter
1 cup chopped yellow onion
1 teaspoon chili powder
1 teaspoon black pepper
½ teaspoon kosher salt
¼ cup granulated sugar
1 tablespoon brown sugar
2 teaspoons sweet paprika

12 hamburger buns

Rub
4 tablespoons chili powder

Braising Liquid
1 cup water
1 large onion, cut in large pieces
2 bay leaves
1 teaspoon kosher salt

Sauce
½ teaspoon ground cumin
½ teaspoon crushed red pepper flakes
2 teaspoons celery salt
1½ cups beef stock
¾ cup cider vinegar
1 cup ketchup
2 tablespoons Worcestershire sauce

While not "barbecue," this recipe makes a good "BBQ" sandwich and is not a bad substitute when the weather is really foreboding as often the case in the Northern climates during the winter months.

Rub roasts with chili powder and pepper. Brown roasts on all sides in hot Dutch oven. Add remaining braising liquid ingredients and bring to boil. Cover and simmer, stirring occasionally, for about three hours until pork is very well done and starts to separate into strings. Remove pork and continue cooking beef another hour or until equally tender. Remove beef from liquid. Shred beef and pork, removing as much fat as possible.

Sauce: In a heavy saucepan, melt butter and add onion. Cook until onion is translucent, about five minutes. Add spices and seasonings, cook until aromatic, about three minutes. Add remaining liquid ingredients and mix well. Simmer over low heat for 30 minutes. Add shredded meats and simmer until thick, about 15 minutes. Serve on warmed hamburger buns with Carolina Slaw (Page 179).

Grilled Beef Kabobs

1½ pounds lean Top Round
¼ cup lemon juice
2 tablespoons Worcestershire sauce
3 tablespoons corn oil
¼ cup soy sauce
2 tablespoons prepared mustard

1 clove garlic, minced
1 green bell pepper, cut into chunks
8 fresh mushrooms
8 cherry tomatoes
2 large red onions, quartered

Make marinade by combining lemon juice, Worcestershire sauce, oil, soy sauce, mustard, and garlic in a medium mixing bowl. Cut beef into one-inch chunks and then put in marinade. Cover and marinate, refrigerated, for 12 hours. Cut vegetables into chunks, making at least eight pieces of each. Remove beef cubes from marinade, reserving marinade. On four long skewers, alternate pieces of meat and vegetables. Grill over hot coals, basting occasionally with reheated marinade, for about 15 minutes, turning skewers regularly. (Allow five to 10 minutes longer for well-done meat.).

Wined Teriyaki Strips

1 (1½-pound) Flank steak
½ cup reduced sodium soy sauce
¼ teaspoon minced garlic
2 tablespoons dark brown sugar
1-inch ginger root, crushed

1 cup dry white wine
1½ tablespoons minced onion
2 tablespoons lemon juice
1 (10½-ounce) can beef broth

Slice steaks diagonally across grain into ¼-inch by 1-inch strips. Place in large bowl. Combine remaining ingredients. Pour over meat and marinate at least an hour, turning three or four times. Thread on skewers and grill over coals until done as desired.

Great Smoky Cheeseburgers

1½ pounds ground chuck	¼ cup Tennessee Gourmet™
1 tablespoon kosher salt	Apple & Spice Sauce
1 tablespoon black pepper	4 ¼-inch slices red onion
½ tablespoon granulated garlic	4 ¼-inch slices tomato
½ tablespoon onion powder	4 large hamburger buns
1 teaspoon celery seed	4 leaves Romaine lettuce
1 tablespoon Worcestershire sauce	4 slices Monterey Jack Jalapeño cheese

What's the difference with ground meats? Ground beef is 73% lean; ground chuck, 80% lean; ground sirloin, 85% lean; and ground round, 90% lean.

In a large mixing bowl, combine hamburger, salt, pepper, garlic, onion powder, celery seed, Worcestershire sauce, and Tennessee Gourmet™ Apple & Spice Sauce (your favorite flavor). Mix thoroughly. Form into four patties, about two inches thick. Refrigerate, covered, until cooking.

Over a medium hot direct grill, cook patties, covered, for about five minutes. Flip and cook another four minutes. Top with red onion and cheese slice. Cover grill and cook another two to three minutes or until burgers reach an internal temperature of 160° F. and cheese is melted. Serve on buns with lettuce and tomato.

Great Smoky Cheeseburger with onion rings and salad

Chicken & Poultry

The U.S. Department of Agriculture Food Safety & Inspection Service inspects poultry, as it does for beef, to insure wholesomeness. Although voluntary, most producers and processors also have their poultry graded by the federal Agricultural Marketing Service.

Poultry has three grades: A, B, and C although usually only Grade A poultry is found in the supermarket. Grade A means the poultry is free from defects like bruises and discoloration and that there are no broken bones. For whole birds and parts with skin, Grade A also means there are no tears in the skin. Poultry necks, wing tips, giblets, and ground poultry are not graded.

Chickens found in the supermarket are: a broiler-fryer, a chicken that is about 7-weeks-old and weighing 2½ to 4½ pounds; a roaster, a five- to seven-pound chicken that is 3- to 5-months-old; a capon, a castrated male chicken weighing four to seven pounds that is usually roasted whole; and Cornish game hen, a small broiler-fryer weighing between one and two pounds that is also usually roasted whole.

Duck: most domestic duck are White Pekin (Long Island duck is a brand name given to ducks raised on Long Island, New York, for at least seven days and processed there). Because duck contains so much subcutaneous fat, the skin is usually scored before cooking. A popular method of cooking Pekin duck is to marinate duck pieces and then steam the duck and finish it on a hot grill. Two other popular ducks are Moulard, which is sold as 1¼-pound breasts and has the gamiest flavor, and Muscovy, which is more flavorful and fatter than Pekin and often used for foie gras. (Peking duck is a method of cooking Pekin duck.)

Basic Instructions

Chicken Breasts (Bone-In Breast Halves)

Roast: Brush with oil, season with salt, pepper, and crushed rosemary. Preheatgrill for indirect cooking and roast, skin side up, at 375° F. 15 to 20 minutes. Turn and roast another 15 to 20 minutes until cooked through and the juices run clear.

Grill: Marinate or rub with seasonings. Grill over medium high direct heat six to eight inches from the coals, skin side up, for 10 to 15 minutes. Turn and grill another 10 to 15 minutes or until juices run clear.

Chicken Breasts (Boneless Breast Halves)

Grill: Marinate or rub with seasonings. Grill over medium high direct heat six inches above the coals, skin side up, for six to eight minutes. Turn and grill another six to eight minutes or to an internal temperature of 165° F. Allow to rest five minutes before serving.

Halves and Quarters

Broiler halves or quarters are the best serving size for individual meals. Start cooking the chicken with the bone side down and turn every 10 minutes. Keep the fire low so that the chicken does not dry out. Allow one to 1½ hours for a well-done barbecue chicken half or quarter. The cooking time will depend on the size of the broiler, the heat of the fire, and the weather conditions. Mop or brush the chicken each time the pieces are turned. Brush with barbecue sauce during the last 20 minutes of cooking.

Whole Chicken

Preheat the grill to medium heat (350° F.). Rinse the chicken and pat dry with paper towels. Season inside and out with salt and pepper. Place chicken, breast side up, on grill and roast, basting occasionally with a poultry mop. Cook until the thigh temperature is 180° F., about 15 to 20 minutes per pound. Allow chicken to rest 10 minutes before carving. (The best method of cooking whole poultry is to use a rotisserie with indirect heat and a drip pan under the bird. Using a rotisserie, a whole three- to four-pound broiler will cook in about 60 to 75 minutes. A five- to seven-pound roasting hen should be cooked for 18 to 25 minutes per pound.)

Cornish Hens

Bake: Preheat indirect grill to medium heat (350° F.). Season hens inside and out with salt, pepper, and crushed rosemary. Place hens on the grill, breast side up, and roast about 45 to 55 minutes.

Grill: Split hens in half and remove backbone. Season the hens with salt, pepper, and rosemary. Grill over medium coals, skin side up, basting occasionally, eight to 10 minutes. Turn, baste, and cook another eight to 10 minutes.

Poultry Preparation

Brine the chicken an appropriate amount of time *(see Brining, Page 22).* Remove from brine, rinse thoroughly, and pat dry.

Apply Italian dressing or a good quality olive oil to both the outside and inside, season with salt, pepper, garlic powder, and crushed rosemary. Add a little thyme or poultry seasoning. Place chicken in a resealable plastic bag and marinate for a few hours in the refrigerator.

To truss whole poultry: Put the breast side up. Loop the middle of a length of butcher's twine, about 2½ feet in length, under the tail and over the end of the drumsticks, tie tightly. Pull the ends toward the front of the chicken; running the twine between the breasts and legs. Turn the bird over and loop the wing joints with the twine bringing it together at the back of the bird. Tie tightly.

Preparing Broilers

Splitting whole broilers is the most economical way to do grilled chicken for a large number of people. A sharp knife, a pair of kitchen shears, and a little time will save quite a bit of money. Reserve the backbones for stock.

Place whole broiler on a poultry cutting board with the wishbone to the back and the breast side down. Use a sharp knife or kitchen shears to cut from the tail along each side of the backbone.

Spread the split back apart about five inches. Cut the breastbone cartilage straight back to the breastbone. Spread the back further apart until the split cartilage gives way and exposes the breastbone.

Separate the breastbone from the broiler by running your thumb down one side of the bone and your index finger down the other side. Separate the rear cartilage portion of the breastbone and remove. Lift the rear portion of the remainder of the breastbone and remove.

How To Flatten Chicken Breasts

The easiest method of getting a uniformly flat chicken breast is to freeze the breast for about 15 minutes and then butterfly the breast to a 3/4-inch thickness. Get two good-size pieces of waxed paper and lightly coat one side with water. Put the breast on the moistened waxed paper, cover with second sheet of waxed paper and uniformly pound with a meat mallet or small skillet.

Cooking Chicken For A Crowd

Aside from a whole pig or a half-dozen beef briskets, chicken halves or quarters make a great cookout/ barbecue for a crowd. Here's a guide adapted from the Mississippi State University Extension Service on cooking chicken halves for a crowd.

Ingredient/Dish	People Served		
	10	**20**	**50**
Chickens (2- to 3-pound)	5	10	25
Potato Chips	12 ounces	1½ pounds	3 pounds
Potato Salad	2 quarts	1 gallon	2½ gallons
Coleslaw	2 quarts	1 gallon	2½ gallons
Pickles	1 pint	1 quart	2 quarts
Soft Drinks	12	24	60
Charcoal	5 pounds	10 pounds	25 pounds
Grills (2 by 3 feet)	1	2	4
Sauce			
Cider Vinegar	1 pint	1 quart	2 quarts
Vegetable Oil	½ pint	1 pint	1 quart
Cayenne pepper sauce	2 teaspoons	4 teaspoons	8 teaspoons
Crushed red pepper flakes	2 teaspoons	4 teaspoons	8 teaspoons
Garlic Powder	¼ teaspoon	½ teaspoon	1 teaspoon
Salt	4 tablespoons	8 tablespoons	1 pound

Prepare the broilers by removing the backbones and splitting the chickens in half. Start cooking the chicken over an open pit or large grill with the bone side down. Keep the fire at a medium (350° F.) temperature and turn every 10 to 15 minutes so the chicken does not scorch. Allow 1½ to two hours for well-done grilled chicken half. The actual cooking time will depend on the height of the pit, the size of the broiler, the heat of the fire, and the weather conditions. Use an instant-read thermometer to be sure the chicken is fully cooked. Mop the chicken each time the broiler is turned.

How Long To Smoke Poultry

A variety of woods can be used to smoke-cook chicken: alder, apple, cherry, and pecan being the most popular. Because of the subtle flavor of chicken, avoid heavy tasting woods such as mesquite or hickory. Smoke chicken halves at 225° F. to 250° F. for about three to 3½ hours. After an hour or so of smoking, brush the skin with a little oil or poultry mop. Mop again after about two hours to keep the chicken from drying out. Smoke bone-in breasts for about two hours. Boneless breasts will be ready in about an hour. Cook whole poultry until the thigh reaches an internal temperature of 180° F. Breasts should cook to an internal temperature of 170° F.

Chicken that is smoked at a low temperature will still show pink around the joints. This may be undesirable for presentation as some people might think the chicken is undercooked although it is properly prepared. To avoid the pink coloring, it is necessary to smoke-cook poultry at a higher temperature (275° F. to 300° F.) for two to three hours.

Barbecue Duck

1 large duck	2 tablespoons Worcestershire sauce
½ cup unsalted butter, melted	½ teaspoon garlic salt
2 tablespoons orange juice	1/2 teaspoon black pepper
1 tablespoon lemon juice	1 yellow onion, quartered
¼ cup chopped yellow onion	1 orange, quartered
½ teaspoon cayenne pepper sauce	

Rinse the duck and pat dry, par-boil in a large stockpot and drain. Dry with paper towels and season with salt and pepper. Combine the butter, juices, chopped onion, cayenne pepper sauce, Worcestershire sauce, garlic salt, and pepper, mixing well. Stuff the ducks with the quartered onion and quartered orange. Make a slit in the lower side of each breast. Place on rack in roasting pan and brush with the butter sauce. Cover with foil and roast in a medium high (375° F.) barbecue for 1½ hours or until tender, basting with sauce every 10 to 15 minutes. Remove foil and roast an additional 20 minutes or until browned.

Grilled Chicken Caesar Salad

4 boneless chicken breasts	½ cup prepared Caesar dressing
1 head Romaine lettuce	¼ cup Parmesan cheese
½ pound sliced mushrooms	½ teaspoon kosher salt
½ cup garlic croutons	½ teaspoon black pepper
2 cloves garlic, crushed	1 teaspoon crushed rosemary
1 medium red onion, sliced	

Tear Romaine into bite-size pieces; combine with mushrooms, croutons, garlic, onion, and Caesar dressing. Place on chilled salad plates. Spoon one teaspoon of Parmesan cheese over each serving and top with cracked black pepper. Refrigerate.

Season the chicken breasts with salt, pepper, and rosemary. Grill over hot coals about five minutes per side. Slice and serve over salad. Garnish with remaining cheese.

Garlic Chicken

4 boneless chicken breasts
4 cloves garlic
1 teaspoon kosher salt
2 tablespoons black peppercorns

½ cup chopped fresh cilantro
2 tablespoons lime juice
1 medium tomato, sliced
4 green onions, made into brushes

Chop the garlic with salt to make a smooth purée. Coarsely crush the peppercorns and combine with the garlic purée, cilantro, and lime juice. Rub the mixture on the chicken, cover and refrigerate at least one hour. Grill chicken over hot coals about six minutes per side. Garnish with tomatoes and green onion brushes.

Lemon Chicken

1 (2- to 2½-pound) chicken
¼ cup lemon juice
¼ cup vegetable oil

½ teaspoon dried thyme
1 teaspoon black peppercorns

Combine lemon juice, oil, and thyme. Coarsely grind or crush peppercorns and add to lemon mixture. Quarter the chicken and place chicken in a shallow non-reactive dish. Pour lemon mixture over chicken. Marinate, refrigerated, for two to three hours, turning occasionally. Cook chicken over hot coals or on a medium-high gas setting, turning frequently, about 25 to 30 minutes on each side or until juices run clear.

Santa Fe Chicken

4 boneless chicken breasts
1 teaspoon seasoned salt
¼ teaspoon black pepper
Romaine lettuce leaves

4 hamburger buns
4 (1-ounce) slices Canadian-style bacon
4 (1-ounce) slices Swiss cheese
Salsa or barbecue sauce

Combine seasoned salt and pepper. Loosen one edge of chicken skin and rub seasoning mixture under skin. Cook chicken, skin-side down, on covered grill over medium indirect heat about eight minutes per side or until chicken is tender and no longer pink. Remove skin. Serve chicken on grilled hamburger buns topped with cheese, bacon slices, lettuce, and salsa (or barbecue sauce).

Spicy Cape Cod Chicken

4 boneless chicken breasts
2 tablespoons unsalted butter
2 stalks celery, finely chopped
½ yellow onion, finely chopped
½ teaspoon crushed rosemary
½ teaspoon black pepper
½ teaspoon kosher salt
¾ cup water

½ cup whole fresh cranberries
¼ cup Tennessee Gourmet™
  Sneaky Hot Sauce
2 cups herb stuffing mix
¼ cup Tennessee Gourmet™
  Snappy Pepper Jelly
¼ cup seasoned bread crumbs

The apple in the gourmet sauce nicely balances the spice and complements the tartness of the cranberries making for a flavorful stuffing. If desired, drizzle finished chicken rounds with a béarnaise or hollandaise sauce or top with rosemary cream sauce.

In a medium saucepan, melt butter over medium heat until butter foams. Add celery, onion, rosemary, black pepper, and salt. Cook until celery is tender, about five minutes. Add water and bring to a low simmer. Add cranberries and cook until berries burst, about four minutes. Mash berries against side of saucepan. Add Tennessee Gourmet™ Sneaky Hot Apple & Spice Sauce and incorporate. Add stuffing mix. Stir well. Cover and remove from heat. Cool for 10 minutes. Fluff stuffing mix, refrigerate and cool completely.

Pound chicken breasts between two sheets of waxed paper until ¼-inch thick. Spread two to three tablespoons of stuffing mix atop each breast and roll up, securing with wooden picks. Be careful not to cross-contaminate stuffing. Place chicken breasts, seam side down, in a buttered baking dish. Brush chicken breasts with Tennessee Gourmet™ Snappy Pepper Jelly. Cover with aluminum foil and bake in 350° F. covered grill for 30 minutes. Uncover, sprinkle with bread crumbs and continue cooking 30 to 45 minutes or until chicken has a 165° F. internal temperature.

Remove from grill and allow to rest, covered, five to 10 minutes. Bias-slice rolled breasts into ½-inch thick rounds. Garnish with fresh rosemary or parsley.

Grilled Key Lime Chicken Breasts

4 boneless chicken breasts
Salt and pepper
½ cup fresh Key lime juice

1 tablespoon olive oil
1 large clove garlic, pressed
1 tablespoon chopped basil

Season the chicken breasts with salt and pepper. Marinate in lime juice, oil, garlic, and basil six hours or overnight. Grill over moderate heat six to seven minutes, turn and cook an additional six to seven minutes.

Spiced Grilled Chicken

1 (2½- to 3-pound) chicken
2 tablespoons olive oil
¼ cup finely chopped onion
1 clove garlic, minced
¾ cup ketchup
1 tablespoon Worcestershire sauce
½ teaspoon celery seed

1 teaspoon Tabasco® sauce
½ teaspoon kosher salt
¼ cup vinegar
2 teaspoons dark brown sugar
1 teaspoon dry mustard
¼ teaspoon black pepper

Heat oil in saucepan and cook the onion and garlic until tender but do not brown. Add ketchup, stir, and add remaining ingredients except chicken. Bring to a boil. Reduce heat, simmer, uncovered, for 10 minutes, stirring occasionally. Set sauce aside.

Quarter the chicken and season with salt and pepper. Place chicken pieces bone side down over medium to hot coals. Grill 25 minutes (until bone side is well browned). Turn pieces over and grill 25 minutes more until chicken is tender. Brush chicken frequently with sauce during last 10 minutes of grilling.

Chili-Rubbed Chicken

1 (3-pound) chicken, quartered

Rub

2 tablespoons dark brown sugar
1 teaspoon ground cayenne

⅓ cup chili powder

Mop

¾ cup ketchup
1 teaspoon cayenne pepper sauce

1 cup hickory barbecue sauce
¼ cup orange juice

For the rub: Mix all ingredients together in bowl.

For the mop: Mix ingredients in saucepan, heat to simmer.

Arrange chicken in a single layer on a baking sheet. Season the chicken with salt and pepper and sprinkle rub on both sides of chicken. Prepare grill for medium-high indirect cooking. Scatter drained alder wood chips over coals. Place chicken, skin side down, on cooking grate on side opposite coals. Cover grill and cook chicken, turning and mopping every 15 minutes, about one hour or until done.

Bring remaining mop sauce to a low simmer and serve with chicken.

Southwestern Chicken Breasts

4 boneless chicken breasts
¾ cup olive oil
¼ cup fresh lime juice
2 tablespoons green chiles

1 teaspoon minced fresh garlic
4 slices Cheddar cheese
Salsa

In a nine-inch square baking pan, stir together oil, lime juice, chiles, and garlic. Add chicken breasts; marinate, refrigerated, at least two hours, turning every 30 minutes. Prepare grill for indirect cooking. Remove chicken from marinade; drain. Grill chicken eight minutes; turn. Continue grilling until thoroughly cooked, about another six to eight minutes. Top each chicken breast with slice of cheese. Cover grill and cook until cheese begins to melt. Serve with salsa.

Grilled Chicken Breasts

4 boneless chicken breasts
2 teaspoons Dijon-style mustard
3½ tablespoons wine vinegar
2 teaspoons minced garlic
2 teaspoons clover honey

1 tablespoon fresh thyme
¼ teaspoon kosher salt
½ teaspoon crushed red pepper flakes
2 tablespoons olive oil

Place the chicken breasts in a folded piece of plastic wrap and flatten the upper portion of each breast with a chef's knife or mallet. Place breasts in a shallow dish. In a small bowl, combine mustard, vinegar, garlic, honey, thyme, salt, and pepper flakes. Add oil a little at a time and whisk to combine. Pour marinade over breasts. Cover with plastic wrap and marinate in refrigerator, turning once or twice, for at least two hours or up to four hours. Remove breasts from marinade. Transfer the marinade to small saucepan and bring to a boil; boil two minutes and reserve. Lightly grease cooking grate with vegetable oil. Place breasts on preheated medium high direct-heat grill. Cook, covered with lid, basting frequently with marinade about six to eight minutes on each side.

Chicken with Sesame-Chile Sauce

1 (2½- to 3-pound) chicken
¼ cup Hoisin sauce
3 tablespoons clover honey
1 tablespoon sesame seed
2 teaspoons grated ginger
½ teaspoon five-spice powder

¾ cup sweet-and-sour sauce
¼ cup reduced sodium soy sauce
¼ cup water
2 cloves garlic, minced
1½ teaspoons chile sauce

Sesame-Chile Sauce: In a small saucepan, combine all of the ingredients except chicken. Cook over medium heat to boiling, stirring frequently. Reduce heat. Cover and simmer for five minutes and reserve.

Quarter chicken, rinse, and pat dry with paper towels. Break wing and drumstick joints so the bird will lie flat during cooking. Twist wing tips under back.

Place chicken, skin side down, on an uncovered grill directly over medium coals for 25 to 30 minutes. Turn and grill 20 to 25 minutes more or until the thigh reaches an internal temperature of 180° F. Brush with sauce frequently during the last 10 minutes of grilling.

Transfer chicken to a serving platter. Heat any remaining sauce and serve with chicken.

Teriyaki Chicken

4 boneless chicken breasts
1 cup teriyaki sauce (Page 56)
¾ cup pineapple juice
½ cup white vinegar
¼ cup Worcestershire sauce
½ cup dark brown sugar, firmly packed

1 teaspoon garlic powder
½ cup Italian salad dressing
½ cup cashew pieces
1 (10-ounce) can crushed pineapple
2 cups uncooked rice

Mix all ingredients except chicken, cashews, pineapple, and rice and bring to a boil. Cool; divide in half. Use half to marinate chicken breasts overnight. Refrigerate other half for later use.

Remove chicken from marinade and discard marinade. While rice is cooking, grill chicken about six minutes per side. Stir drained pineapple and cashew pieces into cooked rice. Reheat reserved marinade. Serve grilled chicken over rice mixture with warmed marinade sauce.

Mesquite-Grilled Chicken with Citrus Sauce

4 boneless chicken breasts	2 lemons, peeled and chopped
1 cup olive oil	2 limes, peeled and chopped
2 cloves garlic, crushed	2 oranges, peeled and chopped
2 tablespoons minced cilantro	2 cups chicken stock
1 tablespoon fresh thyme	1 teaspoon cornstarch
2 green onions, chopped	1 teaspoon water
2 tablespoons unsalted butter	⅓ cup Grand Marnier
2 shallots, minced	½ teaspoon white pepper
1 teaspoon minced fresh ginger	¼ teaspoon kosher salt

In a ceramic or glass bowl, combine the oil, garlic, cilantro, thyme, green onions, and chicken breasts. Marinate, refrigerated, at least eight hours or overnight.

Melt butter in a medium saucepan over medium-low heat, cook the shallots and ginger, stirring, until the shallots soften. Add the chopped lemons, limes, and oranges and simmer for 10 to 12 minutes, or until the liquid is reduced to a syrup-like consistency. Add the stock, increase the heat to medium and boil the mixture, stirring occasionally, for 10 to 15 minutes or until reduced by one-third. Mix the cornstarch and water together. Stir in the cornstarch mixture, bring to boil and simmer the sauce for two minutes. Strain through a fine sieve into a bowl. Add the Grand Marnier Cordon Rouge, white pepper, and salt.

Remove the chicken from the marinade and bring to room temperature. Prepare a medium-hot grill for direct cooking using pre-soaked and drained mesquite chips.

Grill the chicken about five inches above the coals and mesquite, turning it once, for 10 to 12 minutes. Transfer the chicken to a serving dish and spoon the sauce over it.

Jamaican Jerk Chicken

1 chicken, quartered	½ cup red wine vinegar
1 tablespoon dark brown sugar	½ cup white vinegar
1 tablespoon fresh thyme	¼ cup soy sauce
1 teaspoon ground cinnamon	½ cup olive oil
½ teaspoon ground nutmeg	6 green onions, finely chopped
1 teaspoon cracked black pepper	2 shallots, minced
¼ teaspoon cayenne pepper	2 cloves garlic, minced
1 teaspoon kosher salt	1 tablespoon grated ginger
½ cup orange juice	1 Habanero pepper, finely chopped

Combine sugar, herbs, spices, salt, orange juice, vinegars, and soy sauce in medium bowl; slowly mix in the olive oil, whisking constantly to create an emulsion. Add green onions, shallots, garlic, ginger, and Habanero chile. Set aside for an hour.

Rinse chicken and pat dry. Rub jerk sauce under and over chicken skin. Cover and refrigerate at least four hours.

Prepare medium-hot indirect grill. Sear chicken over direct heat, about five minutes per side. Move to indirect heat and cook at 350° F. for one hour, turning and basting with jerk sauce every 15 minutes.

Korean-Style Grilled Chicken

1 broiler-fryer chicken	¼ cup sesame seeds
¼ cup corn oil	¼ cup light (not Lite) soy sauce
¼ cup dark corn syrup	1 small onion, sliced
1 clove garlic, crushed	¼ teaspoon black pepper
¼ teaspoon ground ginger	

Quarter the chicken, rinse and pat dry. In a shallow baking dish, combine the marinade ingredients. Add chicken, turning to coat. Cover and refrigerate, turning once, at least three hours. Grill over medium coals, turning and basting frequently, about one hour.

Grilled Caribbean Chicken Breasts

4 boneless chicken breasts
1 tablespoon grated orange peel
1 tablespoon olive oil
1 tablespoon lime juice
1 teaspoon minced fresh ginger

¼ cup orange juice
2 cloves garlic, minced
½ teaspoon cayenne pepper sauce
½ teaspoon chopped oregano

Place the chicken breasts in a folded piece of plastic wrap; slightly flatten upper portion of each breast. Place breasts in a shallow glass dish. Combine remaining ingredients in a small bowl. Pour marinade over breasts. Cover with food film and marinate, refrigerated, for at least two hours or up to four hours. Remove breasts from marinade. Preheat grill to medium heat and lightly oil cooking grate. Place breasts on grill. Cook chicken breasts, covered, about six to eight minutes on each side.

Peppery Chattanooga Chicken

4 boneless chicken breasts
4 teaspoons lemon juice
¼ teaspoon kosher salt
¼ teaspoon black pepper
½ teaspoon garlic powder

4 tablespoons Tennessee Gourmet™
  Snappy Pepper Jelly
8 slices Havarti cheese
2 tablespoons olive oil

Place breasts between two sheets of waxed paper and pound to a ½-inch thickness. Season the breasts with lemon juice, salt, pepper, and garlic powder. Place one slice of Havarti cheese and one teaspoon Tennessee Gourmet™ Snappy Pepper Jelly in middle of each breast. Fold breast over to form a pocket and secure with wooden picks. Refrigerate, covered, for an hour. Remove from refrigerator and bring to room temperature.

Quickly grill breasts over high heat until golden. Turn and brown on other side. Place browned breasts in buttered casserole dish, cover with a generous layer of pepper jelly and second cheese slice. Bake in a 350° F. covered grill for 10 to 15 minutes.

Grilled Chicken Salad

2 boneless chicken breasts

1 medium red onion, sliced

1 tablespoon Roquefort cheese

¼ teaspoon black pepper

3 tablespoons soy sauce

1 teaspoon dried basil

3 tablespoons balsamic vinegar

2 teaspoons chopped basil

4 cups mixed salad greens

1 medium tomato, cut in wedges

Marinade

4 tablespoons lemon juice

2 cloves garlic, minced

Dressing

2 cloves garlic, crushed

5 tablespoons olive oil

Whisk marinade ingredients together in a mixing bowl and set aside.

Place the chicken on a sheet of plastic wrap and cover it with a second sheet. Pound chicken to a thickness of ½-inch. Transfer the chicken to the marinade bowl and cover. Marinate in refrigerator at least 30 minutes.

Preheat the grill. Place the onion rounds in a single layer on a baking sheet and spray lightly with the vegetable oil, turn over and spray the other side. Remove the chicken from the marinade and place alongside the onion rounds. Grill the onion rounds and the chicken for six minutes per side. Let the chicken cool slightly and slice.

Spread an equal amount of the mixed greens on four chilled salad plates; scatter the onion rounds and the sliced chicken on top. Sprinkle ¾-teaspoon Roquefort cheese over each. Garnish with the tomato wedges. Combine the dressing ingredients in a blender and mix at low speed. Spoon dressing onto the salads or serve it on the side.

Tennessee Fajitas

4 boneless chicken breasts	1 large green bell pepper, sliced
3 tablespoons lime juice	1 large yellow onion, sliced
3 tablespoons Tequila	8 10-inch flour tortillas
2 Jalapeño peppers, sliced	4 – 6 tablespoons Tennessee
2 cloves garlic, minced	Gourmet™ Snappy Pepper Jelly
½ teaspoon ground cumin	1 large green bell pepper, sliced
1 tablespoon Worcestershire sauce	2 cups salsa
1 tablespoon fresh cilantro	2 cups guacamole
1 teaspoon crushed red pepper flakes	2 cups shredded Iceberg lettuce
1 teaspoon kosher salt	2 cups sour cream
½ teaspoon black pepper	2 cups shredded Pepper Jack cheese

Trim chicken breasts of any fat. Slice lengthwise into thin strips and then into three- to four-inch lengths. In a non-reactive bowl, combine lime juice, Tequila, Jalapeños, garlic, cumin, Worcestershire sauce, cilantro, crushed red pepper flakes, salt, and black pepper. Add chicken and marinate, refrigerated, four to six hours.

Prepare a medium-hot grill. Using a griddle accessory or a cast-iron skillet, grill drained chicken, sliced pepper, and onions, turning often, eight to 10 minutes or until chicken is opaque. Remove from grill and keep warm by loosely covering with foil. Place tortillas directly on grill. Brush with Tennessee Gourmet™ Snappy Pepper Jelly and grill 30 to 45 seconds until lightly toasted.

To serve, place chicken strips with peppers and onions on a plate and allow guests to build fajitas. Serve with salsa, guacamole, lettuce, sour cream, and shredded cheese.

Memphis Wraps

1 pound ground chicken
3 cups shredded Chinese (Napa) cabbage
½ cup finely chopped green onions
½ teaspoon black pepper
¼ teaspoon kosher salt

½ cup Tennessee Gourmet™
 Salad Dressing Plus
10 six-inch egg roll wrappers
Oil for deep frying

Tennessee Gourmet™ Salad Dressing Plus makes an excellent dipping sauce for these appetizers. Minced shrimp, turkey, or pork may be substituted for the chicken.

In a medium sauté pan, cook ground chicken until cooked, about five minutes. Remove from sauté pan, drain well, and cool completely. In a medium mixing bowl, combine cooked chicken, cabbage, green onions, pepper, salt, and Tennessee Gourmet™ Salad Dressing Plus. Marinate, in a refrigerator, for two hours. Remove from refrigerator and bring to room temperature.

Place one to two tablespoons chicken/cabbage mixture in the middle of each egg roll wrapper. Wet edges with water, roll, fold, and seal. Heat oil in a turkey fryer to 350° F. and deep-fry wraps in batches of three or four wraps until lightly browned, two to three minutes (or until they float). Carefully remove from oil, drain on wire rack over paper towels, and serve.

Cumberland Plateau Chicken Delight

4 boneless chicken breasts
1 teaspoon kosher salt, divided
1 teaspoon black pepper, divided
8 thick slices French bread
2 tablespoons mayonnaise
½ cup unsalted butter

½ cup Tennessee Gourmet™
 Snappy Pepper Jelly
1 tablespoon lemon juice
½ teaspoon granulated garlic
1 pound grated Jack cheese

Not a barbecue recipe, but a tasty chicken dish for those tired of barbecue!

Preheat oven to 400° F. Cut chicken into lengthwise strips, then into three- or four-inch lengths. Season the chicken with ½-teaspoon kosher salt and ½-teaspoon black pepper. Lightly butter bread slices, top with thin layer of mayonnaise. Using broiler pan or baking sheet, lightly toast bread on both sides. Remove from oven and reduce heat to 350° F.

In a medium sauté pan over medium-high heat, melt butter until it foams, add pepper jelly, lemon juice, garlic powder, ½-teaspoon salt, and ½-teaspoon black pepper. Add sliced chicken and cook until chicken is opaque. Place bread slices in broiler pan or large casserole, top with chicken and sauce. Top each slice with grated cheese and bake until golden brown, 15 to 20 minutes.

The Melting Pot

Can You Take the Heat?

Just as the names of chiles vary, so do their characteristics. Aside from the type of chile (there are more than 200 varieties), heat levels are determined by the age and location of the pod on the plant, the soil, ambient air temperatures, and watering. Chiles take a long time to mature and grow best in warmer climates. A confusing factor... how to spell chile. For the plural, chillies, chilies, and chiles are all acceptable! Talk about bewildering!

When preparing chiles for recipes, the heat can be diminished by removing the seeds and the "rib" membranes that hold 80% of the chile's heat. Be sure to wear food-safe gloves when handling chiles.

Note there is a difference between chili and chile. Chili, with an **i**, is a meal prepared with beef and sometimes beans (if you're not from Texas) and also a seasoning powder. Chile, with an **e**, is a seed pod from a plant.

Some of the more commonly used varieties are:

Chile	Characteristics	Suggested Uses
Anaheim	1 to 2" x 4 to 6" with light-green skin and a tapered end. Mild and sweet.	Perfect for sautéing. A good substitute for sweet green bell peppers.
Ancho	A dried poblano, wrinkled and deep burgundy in color. Medium heat with a rich flavor.	Main chile in mole, other sauces, and chili. Often ground as chile powder.
Arbol (Dried)	¼" x 3" with smooth, light- to medium-red skin, brittle. Very hot with lingering heat.	Use in table sauces, soups, and stews.
Chipotle	A dried and smoked Jalapeño; brown in color and wrinkled. They vary in size. Available dried or in adobo sauce in cans. Deep, smoky flavor; medium to hot.	Reconstitute and add to sauce or chili. Also great for barbecue sauces and mops.
Habanero	1 to 1½" x 1 to 1½" with orange, green, or yellow skin and flesh. One of the hottest of all chiles. The intense heat subsides into its complex, fruity flavor.	Adds depth and authority to sauces. Traditional in jerk sauce. Use sparingly.
Jalapeño	1 to 1½" x 2 to 3" long with dark-green, smooth skin, thick juicy flesh and a bullet shape. Medium hot to hot. A crisp, sweet, chile flavor.	Use in salsas, sliced or pickled for nachos. Serranos are a substitute.

Chile	Characteristics	Suggested Uses
Serrano	½" x 2" to 3" with medium-green, smooth skin, thin flesh and a blunt end. Sharper taste than Jalapeños; the heat is gradual and sharp.	Most popular for fresh salsas; also stuffed for chile rellenos.
Scotch Bonnet	1 to 1½" x 1 to 1½" with orange, red, or yellow skin and flesh. One of the hottest of all chiles. A smoky apple-cherry flavor. Not the same as a Habanero but often called a Habanero.	Used in sauces, marinades, and for a full-flavored hot sauce. Use cautiously.
Thai	¾ to 1" in length, thin and red or green skinned. Very hot.	Packs a kick! Used in Southeast Asia cooking.

Substitutions

Occasionally, you might not have a specific ingredient called for in a recipe. Don't worry! That's what makes cooking fun, experimentation. Here are some common substitutes:

Ingredient	If You Don't Have	Use
Arrowroot	1 tablespoon arrowroot	1 tablespoon cornstarch
Fresh herbs	1 tablespoon fresh herbs	1 teaspoon dried herbs
Garlic	1 medium clove garlic	⅛ teaspoon garlic powder
Ginger	1 teaspoon fresh ginger	¼ teaspoon ground ginger
Horseradish	1½ teaspoons freshly grated	1 tablespoon prepared
Italian seasoning	1 teaspoon Italian seasoning	¼ teaspoon each: oregano, marjoram, and basil, plus ⅛ teaspoon sage
Mustard	1 tablespoon prepared mustard	½ teaspoon ground mustard plus two teaspoons vinegar
Mustard, Chinese	1 tablespoon Chinese hot mustard	½ tablespoon ground mustard plus ½ tablespoon cold water
Onion	1 medium onion, chopped (⅔ cup)	1 tablespoon onion powder or ¼ cup dry minced onion
Poultry Seasoning	1 teaspoon poultry seasoning	¼ teaspoon ground thyme plus ¾ teaspoon ground sage

Measurements & Equivalents

Measurement	Equivalent
3 teaspoons	1 tablespoon
2 tablespoons	1 fluid ounce
2 tablespoons	⅛ cup
4 tablespoons	¼ cup
2 cups	1 pint
4 cups	1 quart
4 quarts	1 gallon
4 cups flour	1 pound unsifted
2¼ cups granulated sugar	1 pound
5 large eggs	1 cup
Juice of 1 lemon	3 – 4 tablespoons
Juice of 1 orange	4 tablespoons
1 cup raisins	6 ounces
1 pound (brick) butter	2 cups
1 stick butter	8 tablespoons (½ cup)
2 tablespoons butter	1 ounce
1 (12-ounce) package cranberries	3 cups
1 medium onion	½ to ⅔ cup chopped

Country-style pork ribs on the smoker

Smoked twice-baked potatoes

Using Deep-Fryers

A southern tradition that is quickly gaining popularity across the country is deep-fried turkey along with the use of "turkey fryers" to prepare other backyard feasts like clam, crawfish, and crab boils.

Turkey fryers – a heavy-duty stand with a high BTU propane burner – are available from a number of sources at a range of prices. Don't purchase an inexpensive cooker, as strength and stability are key safety factors when heating oil. A few words of caution: deep-frying is cooking with a vat of very hot (350° F. to 375° F.) oil so be sure the stand is very sturdy and placed on a level surface away from overhanging branches. Don't use a turkey fryer on a wooden deck and never leave the fryer unattended. Deep-frying is inherently dangerous. If the oil gets above 450° F., it can spontaneously ignite and most turkey fryers do not have thermostats to control the heat. Because of this, Underwriters Laboratory has declined to certify any turkey fryers because of safety concerns.

Manufactured by Superb, this propane-fired burner is ideal for frying turkey and lobster boils.

For the deep-fried turkey, you'll need a high BTU outdoor burner, a 26-quart or 32-quart stockpot with a rack and hanger to lift the turkey and a deep frying thermometer. You'll also need about three gallons of peanut, canola, or sunflower oil. A kitchen syringe, also sold under the brand name of "Cajun Injector," is also necessary to inject the turkey with the marinade. Most barbecue outlets carry injector kits or they may be ordered over the Internet.

A long-sleeved shirt, long pants, closed toed shoes, gauntlet-style asbestos gloves, safety glasses, and a dry chemical fire extinguisher are also a good idea. A caveat... never even think about trying to do this in an enclosed area such as a garage or carport unless you want to invite the fire brigade to dinner.

Cajun Turkey Seasoning Mix

½ cup coarse kosher salt
3 tablespoons onion powder
3 tablespoons black pepper
3 tablespoons white pepper
2 tablespoons dried basil

2 teaspoons ground bay leaf
1 tablespoon ground cayenne pepper
2 teaspoons Filé powder
3 tablespoons granulated garlic
1½ tablespoons hot Hungarian paprika

(Filé powder is ground sassafras.)

Cajun Turkey Marinade

2 ounces liquid garlic
1 ounce liquid crab boil
2 ounces cayenne pepper sauce
½ cup butter, melted

2 ounces onion juice
2 ounces Worcestershire sauce
2 tablespoons Cajun Turkey seasoning

Combine ingredients and inject one ounce per pound of turkey into breast, thighs, and legs.

Turkey Brine

1 gallon cold water
⅔ cup dark brown sugar, firmly packed
1 teaspoon dried thyme
¾ tablespoon cracked allspice
¾ tablespoon crushed juniper berries

⅔ cup coarse kosher salt
½ cup cracked black pepper
1 tablespoon whole cloves
3 bay leaves

Combine herbs, salt, sugar, and two cups water in a medium saucepan and bring to a boil. Reduce heat and simmer for 10 minutes. Add to remaining water and allow the mixture to cool.

Cajun Fried Turkey

1 (12- to 16-pound) brined turkey
Cajun Seasoning mix (See above)

Marinade mix (See above)
Peanut or Canola Oil*

*For a 10- to 12-pound turkey, use 1½ to two gallons of oil; for a 13- to 16-pound turkey, use 2½ to three gallons. If uncertain how much oil to use, place the turkey in the stockpot before seasoning and add water until the turkey is just covered. Use a ruler to measure the distance from the top of the pot to the water level. There should be at least three inches from the top of the pot to the top of the turkey

This is a three-day process but well worth the effort.

After removing the giblets and neck, brine turkey overnight or up to 24 hours. Rinse the turkey well with cold water and pat dry. Place in a large roasting pan and apply the seasoning mix liberally to the inside and outside of turkey. Using a kitchen syringe, inject turkey with marinade (one ounce per pound). Cover pan and refrigerate overnight.

Remove turkey from the refrigerator an hour before cooking to bring to room temperature. Cut the loose skin between the leg and the rib cage, all the way to the hip joint to allow this area to cook fully. Do not truss or tie legs together. Be sure the turkey is *completely dry* to prevent the oil from splattering.

Clip a deep fry thermometer to the side of the stockpot being sure it's submerged by at least one inch of oil. Begin heating oil. Don't set the burner to the highest setting, as you may need to increase the heat after you've added the turkey. Depending on the amount of heat from the burner, this could take 20 minutes to an hour. Do not leave the fryer unattended!

When the oil reaches 365° F., place the turkey on the rack, neck down and *very slowly* lower into the oil. (Always wear gloves and a long-sleeved shirt when doing this. This is best done with two people each holding one side of the hanger. Do not lean over the pot when lowering the turkey.) The oil will bubble quite a bit until the turkey is completely submerged. Check the temperature of the oil; it will drop about 50 degrees when the turkey is lowered into it. Adjust the flame so that the oil returns to 350° F. but do not allow it to go above 375° F. Fry the turkey 2½ to three minutes per pound plus five minutes.

When cooked, carefully remove turkey from the oil. (An instant-read thermometer should register 180° F. in the thickest part of the thigh and 170° F. in the breast.) Place the rack on a small stack of newspapers for a few minutes to drain. Remove turkey from rack and place on a serving platter. Allow to rest for 20 minutes before carving. (Allow one to 1½ pounds of turkey per serving.)

Tempura Batter

1 cup all-purpose flour	1 egg, slightly beaten
¼ cup cornstarch	¾ cup ice water
½ teaspoon kosher salt	¼ cup vegetable oil
1 teaspoon baking powder	1 teaspoon Cajun spice

Tempura is a Japanese method of preparing deep-fried foods. Raw food such as chicken, seafood, or fresh vegetables are sliced and then dipped in a batter made of egg yolks, flour, oil, and water. They are then dropped into 350° F. to 375° F. oil until brown.

Mix together dry ingredients. Add egg, water, and oil. Stir to blend. Add Cajun spice. Use to dip slices of yellow squash, zucchini, eggplant, green tomatoes, onion rings, mushrooms or fish fillets for frying. Batter will keep, covered, and refrigerated, for two days.

Deep-Fry Batter

1 cup all-purpose flour
3 tablespoons cornstarch
½ teaspoon kosher salt
1 tablespoon baking powder

½ teaspoon black pepper
1 (12-ounce) can flat beer
1 tablespoon vegetable oil

Combine dry ingredients, add liquids, and mix well. Use as batter to deep-fry fish, vegetables, or onion rings.

Oklahoma Rib eye

4 Rib eye steaks, 1-inch thick
Steak rub

Oil for deep-frying

Heat oil in a turkey fryer to 375° F. Season steaks with steak rub. Slowly lower steaks into oil and cook 2½ minutes for rare, 4½ minutes for medium rare, or 5½ minutes for medium. Remove from oil and drain three to five minutes before serving.

Hot Wings

3 pounds chicken wings
1 (16-ounce) bottle Italian dressing
4 tablespoons Cajun spice

¾ gallon peanut oil
2 cups chunky blue cheese dressing
Celery sticks

Buffalo Sauce

½ cup margarine
2 cups Wing-Time® Buffalo Sauce
¼ cup dark brown sugar, firmly packed

2 cloves garlic, minced
¼ cup clover honey
2 tablespoons white vinegar

Split wings at joints; discard wing tips (or reserve for stock). Place wing sections in resealable bag, add Italian dressing and marinate, refrigerated, for four hours.

Remove wings from marinade and drain. Put wings into clean resealable bag and add four tablespoons Cajun spice. Shake well to cover wings.

Prepare sauce. In a medium saucepan, melt margarine. Add remaining ingredients and simmer 30 minutes. Keep warm over low heat.

On an outdoor burner, heat oil in 10½-quart pot with strainer basket to 375° F. Dip fry basket into hot oil to coat, remove. Add chicken wings to basket in batches. Slowly lower into oil and cook 10 to 12 minutes. Drain well. Toss wings with Buffalo sauce. Serve with celery and blue cheese dressing.

Pork

Selecting Pork For The Barbecue

Primal pork cuts come from four general areas of a hog: the loin, the leg, the shoulder, and the belly. Each area has its own characteristics making some better for barbecue than others. Unlike beef or chicken, pork is not graded for quality although it is inspected for wholesomeness.

Loin – The backbone of a hog. The loin gives the most tender and leanest cuts including chops, roasts, and cutlets. The loin is further divided into three sections: the rib end (closest to the shoulder), the center cut, and the tenderloin.

Shoulder – The front legs are divided into two sub-primal sections: the butt and the shoulder (or picnic). Due to its high content of fat and low yield, pork shoulder is the most economical cut from a hog. Moist heat cooking produces the best results. The butt is used for pulled pork.

Leg – (the hind section) is sold either whole or half. The three muscles in the leg are sold as the inside round, outside round, and sirloin tip. A shank, also called a butt, comes from the hind leg. The shank is the lower half and the upper part is the butt. A whole ham is the entire hind leg. Moist heat cooking and marinating gives the best results with leg cuts.

Belly – In addition to Spare ribs, the belly is where bacon and side pork are found.

How Much Pork To Cook

The "standard" serving for pork is three ounces of cooked meat. For most pork cuts, start with four ounces of uncooked meat and the yield will be three cooked ounces. Due to their high fat content, Boston butts and pork shoulders are an exception. For those cuts, plan on five to six uncooked ounces for a three-ounce cooked yield.

The following table gives an approximation for estimating pork yield:

Chops & Steaks	Servings Per Pound	Specialty Cuts	Servings Per Pound
Blade Chops	2½ to 3½	Baby Back Ribs	1½
Boneless Chops	4	Spare Ribs	1¼
Loin Chops	2½	Back Ribs	2
Rib Chops	2½	Tenderloin	4
Center Slice Ham	3½		
Roasts			
Leg, Bone-In	3		
Leg, Boneless	4		
Sirloin	2½		
Picnic	3½		

Choosing A Pork Butt For Barbecue

Although sometimes labeled differently, a pork shoulder and a Boston butt are the same thing. The Boston butt comes from the shoulder portion of a pig's front legs and may be boneless, semi-boneless, or bone-in. Most butts are in the six- to nine-pound range.

Boston butts are great pieces of meat for a barbecue. They are very forgiving; as long as the cooking is "in the ball park," you'll end up with good barbecue.

Preparation

Score the fat pad and generously apply a rub, wrap in plastic wrap, and refrigerate overnight. Take the butt out of the refrigerator about an hour before putting it in the smoker or covered grill. When the smoker temperature reaches 230° F. to 235° F., place the butt in the smoker, fat side up, and smoke heavily with hickory or oak for the first four hours.

After four hours of smoking, remove the butt from the grill or smoker and place it in a foil pan, add ½-cup mop and cover with heavy-duty aluminum foil. Return it to the grill or smoker and cook for another four to five hours at between 225° F. and 250° F.

How Long Does it Take?

Pork butt generally takes about 70 minutes per pound, or 8½ to nine hours for a 7½-pound pork butt. The pork butt should come out of the smoker when it is fork tender. For sliceable pork, take it out at an internal temperature of 180° F. For pulled pork, let it cook to an internal temperature of 190° F. Let the butt rest at least 20 minutes before slicing or pulling.

Pork Chops

Grill chops over medium direct heat, placing them directly over hot coals. Cover the grill. Turn chops once and cook to medium doneness. Check for medium doneness by touching the center of the chops, there should be a slight give. Properly cooked chops may have a slight hint of pink in the center but the juices will run clear. Total cooking time depends on the thickness of the chop: a ¾-inch chop should cook six to eight minutes, a one-inch chop for eight to 10 minutes, and 1½-inch chop for 12 to 16 minutes. The internal temperature should be 155° F. when the chops come off the grill.

Pork Tenderloin

Remove the silverskin from the tenderloin. Beginning at the narrow end, work a boning knife under the silverskin and slowly cut toward the thick end of the loin.

Use a dry rub, if desired, to give the tenderloin a nice crust.

Cook pork tenderloin with indirect heat placing meat on the cooking grate away from the coals. Baste frequently with marinade. Turn tenderloin over halfway through the cooking time. Grill until the internal temperature reaches 155° F., about 20 to 25 minutes. Allow meat to rest five to 10 minutes to come to an internal temperature of 160° F. before slicing on a diagonal.

Pork Roast

Grill pork roast over indirect heat placing roast on the cooking grate away from the coals. Season with dry rub and baste with marinade during cooking. Cook until the internal temperature reaches to 155° F., about 15 to 20 minutes per pound, depending on the heat of the fire.

Pit Roasting A Pig (Pig Pickin')

North Carolina is known for its pig pickin' where guests serve themselves by picking cooked meat from the pig. In the eastern part of the state, the entire pig is cooked and a finishing sauce is made with vinegar and pepper. In the western part of North Carolina, Boston butts are cooked and a vinegar and tomato finishing sauce is used. Coleslaw, boiled potatoes, hush puppies, and sweet iced tea always accompany the feed.

First, you need to figure how big a pig you need. A 75-pound dressed pig will give about 30 pounds of cooked and chopped meat... enough for about 50 people; a 100-pound pig, about 40 pounds; and a 125-pound pig about 50 pounds or enough for 80 people. For 20 people – a small gathering by pig pickin' standards – you'll need a dressed pig weighing about 40 pounds. Plan ahead; it usually takes a week or more to get a fresh pig from a butcher. Have the butcher either split the pig's backbone so it will lie flat on the wire screens or, if you have a small pit, remove the backbone leaving two halves for the barbecue.

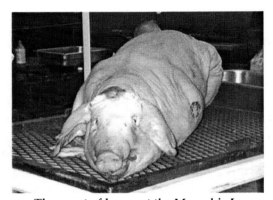

The guest of honor at the Memphis In May barbecue competition
(Courtesy David Klose)

If you've never done a pig before, you'll need to construct a few things... a pit for the cooking and wire screens to hold the guest of honor. Construct two wire screens from half-inch iron pipe covered with a one-inch mesh hardware screen. Build a pit about five feet long and 40 inches wide using three courses of concrete block making it about 16 inches deep. (Obviously, the size of the pit depends on the size of the pig. You want the pit to be a foot or so longer than the pig and about a foot or so wider.) For a 40-pound pig, you'll need about 60 pounds of lump charcoal for the entire barbecue. Start with about 25 pounds of charcoal in a pit alongside the pig pit. If you have any oak or hickory logs, throw them in with the charcoal. When the charcoal forms a nice coating of gray ash, shovel it into the pig pit placing more under where the shoulders and butt will cook. Add more charcoal and hardwood to the side pit to keep a ready supply of hot coals.

Rub the inside of the pig with kosher salt and cracked black pepper. Place the pig over the pit bone side down. Cook one hour then baste (See Page 58 for a basic vinegar mop) and turn the carcass by placing one screen on top of the pig, grasping both handles (with a helper on the other end) and quickly inverting.

Roast the pig adding three to five pounds of pre-burned charcoal and turning every hour. Cook until the pig reaches an internal temperature of 190° F. which should take anywhere from four to 12 hours, depending on the size of the carcass. Estimate the pig will need to cook on an open pit one hour for every 10 pounds dressed weight. The pig will more require frequent basting and turning to prevent charring as the meat becomes more cooked.

To serve, split the skin down the middle of the back and lay the skin off to each side. Scrape off the subcutaneous fat and pick the meat off the bones with a serving fork. Chop the meat with two cleavers and place in serving pans, drizzle with sauce. Serve with cranberry sauce, candied sweet potatoes, coleslaw, relishes, hot rolls, and corn on the cob.

Barbecue, The Western North Carolina Way

OK. We've got the Eastern North Carolina-style pig pickin' figured out... now it's time to move west where the pig pickin' changes somewhat. Instead of an open pit, barbecue is usually done in 55-gallon drums that have been sawn in half and had a couple of hinges welded in place to keep the sections together. Some cooks, unbelievably, actually use commercial smokers to prepare barbecue!

Western North Carolina barbecue uses Boston butts, not whole pigs, and the sauce has a healthy tablespoon or two of tomato base added to the vinegar and spice base; in the

This custom-built smoker by Ken's Custom Pits features an 18-inch chamber and an upright smoker with four trays

Lexington area it's usually one part ketchup for three parts vinegar while further west one will find equal parts vinegar and ketchup or two parts ketchup for one part vinegar.

Again, figure out how much meat you need. A six- to seven-pound uncooked Boston butt will yield about three pounds of cooked meat or enough for 16 three-ounce servings. Figuring two servings per pig picker, a single butt will serve eight people.

Put a few handfuls of charcoal in the firebox, light them and let them burn down to coals. Then add hickory wood chips – two parts wet (soaked and drained) wood to one part dry – adjust the dampers and vents, and put the butts, fat side up, in the cooking chamber. Put a drip pan half-filled with cider vinegar beneath the meat. Add a half-dozen whole heads of coarsely chopped garlic and a couple of coarsely chopped yellow onions to the drip pan.

Keep the temperature between 225° F. to 240° F. throughout the smoking process. Keep the firebox fed and a good smoke going for four to five hours. After that, begin mopping the butts with a vinegar mop and continue cooking. Figure about 1½ to two hours per pound total cooking time. By the time the barbecue is finished, the outside of the pork will have a dark brown crust. For a good pull-able shoulder, you want the internal temperature to be between 190° F. and 200° F.

When the meat is done, let it cool enough to handle and pull it into thumb-sized chunks discarding as much fat as possible. Put the meat in a Dutch oven, add sauce and let the meat simmer, stirring frequently, until serving.

Cajun Pork Roast

1 (2 ½- to 3-pound) boneless pork roast

Cajun Rub

3 tablespoons sweet paprika
½ teaspoon ground cayenne pepper
1 tablespoon granulated garlic
2 teaspoons dried oregano
2 teaspoons dried thyme

½ teaspoon kosher salt
½ teaspoon white pepper
½ teaspoon ground cumin
¼ teaspoon grated nutmeg

1 (12-ounce) can beer
¼ cup vegetable oil
2 cloves garlic, chopped
2 tablespoons unsalted butter
2 Jalapeños, finely chopped

Mop

½ cup cider vinegar
½ medium yellow onion, finely chopped
1 tablespoon Worcestershire sauce
2 tablespoons dry mustard

Combine rub ingredients in mixing bowl. Apply liberally to roast. Mix mop ingredients together in medium saucepan, bring to boil, reduce heat and simmer 10 minutes.

Prepare grill for indirect cooking. Place roast on rotisserie spit and secure with butcher's twine and skewers. Put drip pan under the roast. Roast 30 minutes per pound or until internal temperature is 160° F., about 1½ hours. Baste every 30 minutes with mop.

Remove roast from spit, allow meat to rest 10 minutes before carving into thin slices.

Pork Tenderloin with Grilled Onions

1 (1½-pound) pork tenderloin	¼ teaspoon dried oregano
1 tablespoon chili powder	1 clove garlic, minced
¼ teaspoon ground cumin	1 large sweet onion, sliced
¼ teaspoon kosher salt	Olive oil cooking spray

Combine chili powder, cumin, salt, oregano, and garlic in small mixing bowl. Sprinkle spice mixture over meat, pressing into surface. Arrange coals for indirect cooking. Place meat on grill, cover and grill for 30 to 45 minutes until thermometer registers 160° F. Spray onion slices with olive oil cooking spray and place on the grill rack over coals the last 10 to 15 minutes of grilling time.

Honey and Herb Grilled Pork Roast

1 (3-pound) boneless pork loin	1 cup beer
½ cup clover honey	½ cup Dijon-style mustard
¼ cup olive oil	½ small yellow onion, finely chopped
1 garlic clove, minced	2 teaspoons dried rosemary
½ teaspoon kosher salt	¼ teaspoon black pepper

Combine all ingredients, except pork roast. Put pork roast in large plastic bag or plastic container. Pour marinade over pork. Marinate at least four hours in refrigerator or overnight. Remove pork roast from marinade, reserving marinade. Grill, covered, for 30 minutes per pound, basting occasionally. Simmer remaining marinade at least five minutes. Drizzle over sliced roast and serve.

Honey Apple Grilled Pork Chops

4 pork loin chops	1½ cups apple cider
¼ cup lemon juice	¼ cup soy sauce
2 tablespoons honey	1 clove garlic, minced
½ teaspoon black pepper	

Combine all ingredients except pork chops. Mix well. Place chops in a shallow dish; pour marinade over chops. Cover and refrigerate overnight, turning occasionally. Remove pork chops from marinade. Grill six inches above medium coals for 10 to 15 minutes, turning and basting with reheated marinade every few minutes.

Smoked Pork with Herbs

1 (1½-pound) pork tenderloin
½ cup white vinegar

1 quart water

Marinade

¼ cup Dijon-style mustard
¼ cup olive oil
½ teaspoon black pepper
3 cloves garlic, pressed
½ teaspoon kosher salt

1 cup beer
¼ cup honey-sweetened mustard
2 teaspoons dried rosemary
½ medium yellow onion, finely chopped

Rub

1½ tablespoons brown sugar
1½ teaspoons hot paprika
½ teaspoon ground cayenne

1½ tablespoons black pepper
1 tablespoon sweet paprika

Soak pork tenderloin in a solution of one-quart water and ½-cup white vinegar for 10 to 15 minutes, rinse, and dry well.

Mix marinade ingredients together to form a smooth mixture, transfer to a large re-sealable plastic bag, add tenderloin and marinate, refrigerated, at least three hours. Remove from refrigerator and pat dry. Mix rub ingredients in small bowl, cover entire tenderloin with rub, and let stand at room temperature for 30 minutes.

Prepare grill or smoker to 225° F. to 250° F. and add a handful of soaked and drained apple wood chips. Remove tenderloin from marinade, reserving marinade. Barbecue using indirect heat for three to 3½ hours or to an internal temperature of 155° F. Add additional charcoal and wood chips as needed to keep grill temperature in the 225° F. to 250° F. range. Drain marinade into saucepan, bring to low boil, and cook five minutes. Baste tenderloin every 30 minutes with the reheated marinade.

Allow tenderloin to rest for five minutes then bias-slice tenderloin across grain and serve with barbecue sauce.

Andouille Sausage

1 (5-pound) boneless pork butt,
   cut into 1-inch pieces
1½ teaspoons chili powder
½ cup Cajun spice
1 teaspoon ground cumin
2 teaspoons garlic powder
¼ cup chopped garlic

¼ cup sweet paprika
3 teaspoons black pepper
1½ teaspoons crushed red pepper flakes
2 teaspoons kosher salt
1½ teaspoons Filé powder
4 to 6 feet sausage casing

Filé powder is ground sassafras often used in Cajun and Creole cooking.

In a mixing bowl, toss the pork with the remaining ingredients. Cover and refrigerate for 24 hours. Remove from the refrigerator and pass the meat through a meat grinder with a ½-inch die. Remove half of the meat and pass through the grinder a second time. Stuff half of the sausage into 1½-inch casings. Tie the casings at four-inch intervals for individual links. Form the remaining mixture into four-ounce patties. Smoke Andouille at 195° F. to 220° F. over hickory or pecan wood for about four to five hours.

Maple-Glazed Pork Chops

4 boneless center cut pork chops
¼ cup plus 2 tablespoons
   pure Vermont maple syrup
4 tablespoons olive oil, divided
3 tablespoons balsamic vinegar
2 green onions, thinly sliced

2 tablespoons chopped juniper
1 tablespoon minced fresh sage
2 teaspoons minced garlic
4 bay leaves, crumbled
1 teaspoon black pepper

Combine ¼-cup syrup, three tablespoons oil, two tablespoons vinegar, green onion, juniper berries, sage, garlic, bay leaves, and pepper in a resealable container. Add chops and marinate, refrigerated, at least six hours or overnight. Drain chops, sprinkle with kosher salt, and grill in a covered grill over medium-high heat 12 to 16 minutes, turning once.

Mix remaining syrup, oil, and vinegar together. Brush chops with syrup mixture and grill, covered, another two to three minutes.

Smoked Pork Chops

4 bone-in center cut pork chops
½ teaspoon ground cloves
½ teaspoon ground coriander
½ teaspoon ground cinnamon
2 tablespoons melted butter
¼ cup olive oil
1 tablespoon Worcestershire sauce

½ teaspoon ground allspice
2 tablespoons clover honey
2 tablespoons soy sauce
1 teaspoon grated orange peel
2 tablespoons ground Chipotle pepper
½ cup chopped fresh cilantro

Combine all ingredients, except chops. Put chops in large plastic bag or plastic container. Pour marinade over pork. Marinate at least four hours in refrigerator, or overnight. Remove pork from marinade, reserving marinade. Smoke chops two to three hours at 220° F. over apple or oak. Alternately, grill chops, covered, five to six minutes per side or to an internal temperature of 160° F. Simmer remaining marinade for five minutes. Drizzle over chops before serving.

Western Carolina-Style Pulled Pork

1 (5-pound) boneless pork butt

Sauce

3 tablespoons unsalted butter
¾ cup chopped sweet onion
2 cups ketchup
1 tablespoon Worcestershire sauce

½ cup cider vinegar
¾ cup dark brown sugar, firmly packed
½ cup prepared mustard
1 tablespoon cayenne pepper sauce

Prepare a medium fire in a covered grill. Smoke pork shoulder with soaked and drained hickory chips; adding more charcoal and wood chips to maintain a medium-low heat – between 200° F. and 225° F. – and smoke until internal temperature of pork is 185° F., about five to six hours. Remove from heat and allow pork to rest 10 minutes before shredding.

In a medium saucepan over medium heat, melt the butter and cook the onion until sweated. Add remaining ingredients and bring to low boil. Reduce heat and simmer 20 minutes.

Pile shredded pork on hamburger buns, top with warmed sauce and serve.

Carolina-Style Pulled Pork

1 (5-pound) boneless pork butt

Rub

2 tablespoons sweet paprika

2 teaspoons ground cayenne pepper

2 tablespoons kosher salt

1 tablespoon black pepper

Baste

1 tablespoon black pepper

2 tablespoons dark molasses

1 cup water

2 tablespoons kosher salt

1 teaspoon ground cayenne pepper

½ cup straight Bourbon whiskey

1½ cups cider vinegar

2 to 4 Chipotle chiles, chopped

1 tablespoon crushed red pepper flakes

Combine rub ingredients in a small bowl. Season pork shoulder with rub; wrap with food film and refrigerate up to 24 hours. Prepare a medium fire in a covered grill. Smoke pork shoulder with soaked and drained hickory chips; adding more charcoal and wood chips to maintain a medium-low heat – between 200° F. and 225° F. – and smoke until internal temperature of pork shoulder is 185° F., about five to six hours. Baste the shoulder every 20 to 30 minutes during the last couple of hours of cooking. Boil any remaining basting sauce for five minutes, shred pork, and sauce with remaining basting liquid.

Grilled Ham Steak & Tennessee Redeye Gravy

1 (½-inch thick) ham steak

2 tablespoons unsalted butter

4 tablespoons strong black coffee

¼ cup Tennessee Gourmet™

Snappy Pepper Jelly

Using the grill's side burner, melt butter in a cast iron skillet and fry ham until done. Remove ham to a platter and cover loosely with foil to keep warm. Add coffee and Tennessee Gourmet™ Snappy Pepper Jelly to the fat; bring to a boil. Serve gravy with the ham, Southern biscuits, and grits.

Lu'au Pork Teriyaki

1 (1½-pound) pork tenderloin

1 cup sliced pineapple in syrup

½ cup teriyaki sauce (Page 56)

¼ cup chopped green onion

½ teaspoon ground ginger

¼ teaspoon garlic powder

1 cup uncooked rice

Drain pineapple, reserving all syrup. Blend syrup, teriyaki sauce, green onions, ginger, and garlic powder, pour over pork and pineapple. Cover and refrigerate at least an hour. Cook rice according to package directions and prepare grill. Remove pork from marinade and grill about six inches from hot coals for about 30 to 40 minutes, turning once, or until pork reaches an internal temperature of 155° F. Pour pineapple and remaining marinade into large sauce-pan. Bring to a boil. Remove from heat and serve pork with sauce and pineapple over rice.

Barbecue Pork Roast

1 (3-pound) boneless pork loin	½ teaspoon black pepper
1 tablespoon ground sage	1 tablespoon seasoned salt
1 teaspoon ground allspice	1 cup chunky applesauce
1 teaspoon ground coriander	½ cup dark brown sugar, firmly packed
1 teaspoon grated nutmeg	

Combine sage, allspice, coriander, nutmeg, pepper, and seasoned salt in spice grinder. Pulse until spices are combined.

Pat pork roast dry and score the fat cap. Press rub mixture into roast. Roast with indirect heat in a covered grill, using hickory or mesquite, until 155° F. internal temperature, about 90 minutes.

During the last 30 minutes of roasting, combine applesauce and brown sugar and coat top of roast. Continue roasting until internal temperature is 160° F. Remove roast from grill and let rest for 10 minutes before carving.

Pork Kabobs

2 pounds pork shoulder, cut into 1-inch cubes	½ teaspoon kosher salt
¾ cup peanut oil	1 teaspoon Italian herbs
¼ cup cider vinegar	3 green bell peppers, cut into 1-inch pieces
1 garlic clove, crushed	1 (16-ounce) can pineapple chunks

Place pork cubes in a non-reactive bowl. In a medium mixing bowl, combine oil, vinegar, garlic, salt, and herbs, blend well, and pour over pork cubes. Cover and refrigerate for four hours or overnight. Drain marinade into a medium saucepan. Bring marinade to a low boil and simmer five minutes. Thread pork cubes, peppers, and pineapple chunks alternately on metal or pre-soaked wooden skewers. Brush with marinade and grill over medium coals for 30 to 40 minutes, turning often and brushing with reheated marinade.

Barbecue Pork Strips

2 pounds boneless pork loin

Marinade

1 teaspoon five-spice powder
2 tablespoons Sake or Mirin
1 tablespoon minced garlic
1 tablespoon Hoisin sauce

2 tablespoons soy sauce
2 tablespoons granulated sugar
1 tablespoon brown bean sauce
1 tablespoon red bean curd paste

Basting Liquid

3 tablespoons boiling water

3 tablespoons maltose or
2 tablespoons honey

Cut pork loin in half. Cut the two halves into ¾-inch strips. Put the strips in a bowl with the marinade and mix well to coat. Marinate overnight in the refrigerator. Remove the pork from the marinade and baste the strips with the malt sugar mixture. Use curved skewers to hang the meat from the top shelf of smoker over a large pan filled with water to at least ½-inch. Smoke the pork at 350° F. for 45 minutes, basting occasionally with the malt sugar. Increase the heat to 425° F. and roast for 20 minutes to finish.

Oriental Pork Tenderloin

1 (1½-pound) pork tenderloin
½ cup sesame oil
1 tablespoon grated fresh ginger

1¼ cups soy sauce
4 garlic cloves, minced
1 cup pork barbecue sauce

Trim pork tenderloin. Combine ¼-cup soy sauce, ¼-cup sesame oil, three minced garlic cloves, and ginger in a deep bowl, mix well. Place pork into marinade and refrigerate for six hours or overnight. Remove pork from marinade and place on preheated grill. Cover grill and smoke-cook 45 to 60 minutes or to an internal temperature of 155° F., turning once. Allow pork to rest for five minutes before slicing.

Prepare sauce: Combine barbecue sauce, ¼-cup sesame oil, ¼-cup soy sauce, and one minced garlic clove in a bowl and mix well. Drizzle over sliced pork.

Chinese Barbecue Pork

1 (1½-pound) pork tenderloin

Marinade

½ teaspoon Asian sesame oil
2 tablespoons Hoisin sauce
1 tablespoon black bean sauce
1½ teaspoons dark brown sugar
Pinch five-spice powder

2 tablespoons soy sauce
1 tablespoon sherry
1½ teaspoons minced ginger
1 clove garlic, minced

Trim any fat and silverskin off the tenderloin; tuck ends under and tie each with butcher's twine. Place in a shallow glass dish.

Whisk together marinade ingredients. Pour marinade over tenderloin and turn to coat. Cover and refrigerate for at least four hours; turning occasionally. Let stand for 30 minutes at room temperature before cooking.

Place tenderloin on rack in roasting pan, reserving marinade. Pour one cup of water into pan. Barbecue, basting generously at least four times, in a medium hot (350° F.) indirect heat grill for 50 to 60 minutes, or until meat thermometer registers 155° F. and meat still has a hint of pink. Remove to cutting board and tent with foil. Let stand for 10 minutes. Remove butcher's twine and, using a sharp knife, slice pork diagonally into thin slices.

Variations:

Thai Barbecue Pork: Substitute fish sauce (Nouc Mâm) for soy sauce and lime juice for sherry. Increase ginger root to one tablespoon. Substitute one tablespoon chopped fresh cilantro for five-spice powder.

Szechuan Barbecue Pork: Substitute one-teaspoon Chinese chili paste for five-spice powder. Add one green onion, chopped.

Smoked Pork Tenderloin

1 (1½-pound) pork tenderloin
1 tablespoon crushed red pepper flakes
2 bay leaves, crumbled
½ teaspoon dried sage

2 tablespoons dark molasses
4 cloves garlic, minced
1 teaspoon dried thyme
¼ cup straight Bourbon whiskey

Combine all ingredients, except tenderloin. Put tenderloin in large food-safe plastic bag or plastic container. Pour in marinade. Marinate, refrigerated, at least four hours or overnight. Remove pork from marinade and bring to room temperature. Smoke-cook tenderloin over apple, hickory, or cherry wood 2½ to three hours at 225° F. or to an internal temperature of 155° F.

Chopped Barbecue Pork

1 (2½-pound) boneless pork roast	½ to ¾ cup white vinegar
2 tablespoons crushed red pepper flakes	2 cups Carolina-style barbecue sauce
2 teaspoons kosher salt	2 yellow onions, finely chopped
1 teaspoon cracked black pepper	1 green bell pepper, chopped

Rinse the pork roast and pat dry with paper towels. Combine the crushed red pepper flakes, salt, and black pepper. Rub the mixture into all sides of the pork. Cover with food film and refrigerate overnight. Place the seasoned pork in a shallow roasting pan and let stand at room temperature an hour. Preheat the grill to medium (350° F.). Pour the vinegar (to taste) over the pork (more for a sharper flavor, less for a mellower flavor). Scatter the chopped onions and bell peppers into the pan. Roast the meat until a thermometer inserted into the thickest part of the roast registers 155° F. Remove roast from grill and let stand one hour, reserving the pan juices. Chop or pull meat into shreds. Heat the barbecue sauce in a large saucepan over a low heat until hot. Skim the fat from the pan drippings and add the drippings to the barbecue sauce. Stir the pork, onions, and bell peppers into the sauce and warm, without boiling, until heated through.

Tasso

1 (8-pound) boneless pork shoulder	5 tablespoons kosher salt
5 tablespoons ground cayenne pepper	3 tablespoons cracked black pepper
3 tablespoons white pepper	2 tablespoons sweet paprika
2 tablespoons ground cinnamon	2 tablespoons chopped garlic

Tasso is a spiced Cajun ham.

Trim the pork of excess fat and cut into one-inch thick, four-inch long strips. Mix seasoning together and place in shallow pan. Roll each pork strip in seasoning and place on wire tray. Cover with plastic wrap and refrigerate overnight or up to two days.

Smoke pork strips over pecan wood in a covered grill or smoker five to seven hours or until pork reaches an internal temperature of 160° F. Cool completely and refrigerate.

Grilled Pork Chops with Habanero Cherry Sauce

4 center cut pork loin chops	1 tablespoon minced garlic
¼ cup dark brown sugar, firmly packed	1 bay leaf
¼ cup Dijon-style mustard	1 teaspoon black pepper
¼ cup soy sauce	¾ cup port wine
8 tablespoons butter, divided	1 pound fresh dark sweet cherries, pitted
1 carrot, finely chopped	1 Habanero chile, minced
1 celery stalk, finely chopped	3 cups chicken stock
½ yellow onion, chopped	Kosher salt
1 tablespoon grated fresh ginger	Cracked black pepper
2 sprigs fresh thyme	2 tablespoons cornstarch
1 tablespoon minced shallot	1 tablespoon water

Combine the brown sugar, mustard, and soy sauce and mix well. Spread the mixture evenly over the chops and marinate, covered and refrigerated, for four to five hours. Remove from refrigerator and bring to room temperature. Drain chops, discarding marinade.

Melt one tablespoon of butter in a non-reactive pan and cook the carrot, celery, onion, ginger, thyme, shallots, garlic, bay leaf, and pepper until the onion turns golden brown. Add the wine, heat and reduce until thick. Add the pitted cherries and the Habanero chile and cook until all the juices are extracted from the cherries. Add the stock, bring to a boil, then reduce the heat, and simmer for 45 minutes. Remove from the heat and strain through a fine sieve, pressing to extract all the juices. Return the strained liquid to a pan over low heat and whip in the remaining butter, one tablespoon at a time. Dissolve the cornstarch in one tablespoon of water and add to the sauce. Heat and stir until the sauce thickens. Season with salt and pepper. Keep the sauce warm.

Prepare a medium-high direct grill, cook the pork chops about eight minutes per side. Serve with warm sauce.

Tropical Grilled Pork

1 (1½-pound) pork tenderloin

Marinade

½ cup good quality olive oil
8 garlic cloves, peeled and sliced
1 tablespoon soy sauce
2 teaspoons rice wine
1 teaspoon five-spice powder

1 teaspoon kosher salt
¾ cup Hoisin sauce
¼ cup granulated sugar
½ cup World Harbors®
    Maui Mountain Tropical BBQ Sauce

Glaze

1 (7½-ounce) container maltose sugar
¼ cup hot water
2 teaspoons Sake or Mirin

½ cup World Harbors®
    Maui Mountain Tropical BBQ Sauce

Prepare the marinade: Heat the oil in a saucepan over medium-high heat. Add the garlic and gently fry just until golden brown (about two minutes). Remove the garlic and discard. Pour the garlic oil into a large mixing bowl, let cool. Stir in remaining ingredients with the garlic oil and mix into a smooth sauce. Allow to cool.

Add the tenderloin and marinate for about an hour. Preheat grill to high (500° F.). Remove the meat from the marinade; boil marinade for five minutes and reserve. Sear tenderloin over direct heat for eight minutes, turn, and sear the other side for eight minutes longer. Reduce the grill temperature to medium (350° F.), brush the pork with the reserved marinade and roast with indirect heat for an additional 25 to 30 minutes, turning once. Remove from grill and let tenderloin rest for five minutes. Slice the pork into ¼-inch slices.

Prepare the glaze: Soften maltose sugar by placing the uncovered container in a microwave oven at high setting for 30 to 45 seconds. Carefully transfer the softened maltose into a double boiler with the water, barbecue sauce, and Sake; mix well. Bring glaze to simmer and keep warm over low heat until ready to use. Spoon a few tablespoons of the glaze over pork before serving.

Hermitage Rotisserie Pork Loin

1 (3-pound) boneless pork loin	2 cups cider vinegar
2 cups water	2 yellow onions, chopped

Marinade

¼ cup Creole mustard	¼ cup Tennessee Gourmet™
2 tablespoons honey	Apple & Spice Sauce

Spice Rub

¼ cup dark brown sugar, firmly packed	2 teaspoons garlic powder
1 teaspoon kosher salt	2 teaspoons dry mustard
1 teaspoon black pepper	1 teaspoon Spike® seasoning

Spike® is an all-natural mixture of 39 herbs, spices, and vegetables. It is available at health food stores and in some supermarket spice sections.

Mix mustard, honey, and gourmet sauce. Apply to pork and marinate, covered and refrigerated, four to six hours or overnight. Remove from refrigerator, liberally apply spice rub incorporating it into the marinade. Let roast come to room temperature, about an hour.

Prepare grill for indirect rotisserie cooking. Place pork loin on spit and secure. Cook over drip pan filled with two cups water, two cups vinegar, and chopped onions, one to 1½ hours or to an internal temperature of 155° F. (Do not allow drip pan to run dry.) Remove roast from grill and allow to rest 10 minutes. Slice on bias into ¼-inch slices and serve with extra sauce for dipping.

Pork Tenderloin with Hawaiian Sauce

1 (1½-pound) pork tenderloin	4 cloves garlic, minced
4 cups reduced beef stock	2 tablespoons prepared horseradish
½ cup Creole mustard	1 teaspoon kosher salt
½ cup prepared (yellow) mustard	1 teaspoon cumin seed
1 tablespoon clover honey	1 teaspoon black pepper
2 tablespoons ketchup	1 (8-ounce) can pineapple rings
2 tablespoons dark brown sugar	

Drain pineapple rings, reserving juice. In a medium saucepan, combine beef stock, reserved pineapple juice, Creole and prepared mustards, honey, ketchup, brown sugar, and garlic. Bring to low simmer and cook until reduced by one-half, remove from heat and add horseradish.

Rub tenderloin with salt, cumin, and black pepper. Grill, basting frequently and turning once, about 20 to 30 minutes with medium indirect heat. Grill pineapple rings during the last 15 minutes of the cooking time and serve with the sliced tenderloin.

Mesquite Grilled Chops with Apple Salsa

4 bone-in center cut pork chops
1 (16-ounce) jar chunky applesauce
1 small red onion, finely chopped
1 Jalapeño pepper, finely chopped

1½ teaspoons granulated garlic
½ teaspoon kosher salt
1 teaspoon white pepper
1 cup mesquite chips

Combine applesauce, onion, Jalapeño, 1-teaspoon granulated garlic, salt, and ½-teaspoon white pepper in a medium bowl. Place chops in resealable bag, cover with one half of the apple salsa and refrigerate at least four hours or overnight. Reserve remaining salsa.

Soak wood chips in water for an hour, drain and put in foil packets or smoker tray. Remove chops from marinade and drain. Season chops with remaining granulated garlic and white pepper. Preheat grill for medium-high direct cooking. Place mesquite packets on lava rocks or briquettes and begin smoking. Add chops and grill, covered, seven to eight minutes per side. Serve with reserved salsa.

Spicy Satay Kabobs

2 pounds pork loin, cut into 1½-inch cubes
1 teaspoon ground coriander
½ teaspoon ground cayenne pepper
½ teaspoon black pepper
1 garlic clove, minced
1 tablespoon dark brown sugar

¼ cup smooth peanut butter
1 teaspoon kosher salt
1 teaspoon ground cumin
4 yellow onions, finely chopped
1½ teaspoons lemon juice
1 tablespoon soy sauce

Put all the ingredients into a large bowl, mix well, and cover. Refrigerate for several hours, mixing occasionally. Put meat cubes on skewers, keeping as much of the onion mixture on them as possible. Grill over medium-hot coals, turning to brown each side, for 10 to 55 minutes or until meat is cooked through.

Chile-Seared Shrimp served with crab cake (recipe page 169)

Smoked pork tenderloin, garlic mashed potatoes, and roasted beefs (recipe page 142)

Ribs, Racks & Slabs

What Type Of Rib?

Which rib to cook is more a matter more of personal preference than dictum. Some argue only Spare ribs are worthy of barbecue as Back ribs are too lean; others contend Back ribs or Baby Backs (ribs from young hogs) make for a better barbecue because they are leaner and have more meat than Spares.

What's the difference? Primarily size and the amount of meat and fat on the rib. Back ribs have at least eight ribs; a full slab has 13 ribs. Backs come from the blade and center section of the loin and are sold as 1½ down (a slab weighing less than 1½ pounds), 1½ – 1¾, 1¾ – 2¼, and 2¼ up. Spare ribs are from a hog's belly and contain 11 to 13 ribs including the breastbone. They are sold 3½ down, 3½ – 5½, and 5½ up. (St. Louis ribs are a different cut of Spare ribs.) Country-style ribs are cut from the upper portion of the pork shoulder and are not true ribs.

The two most important factors for cooking any type of barbecue, including ribs, are time and temperature. The right time and the correct cooking temperature will most often produce good barbecue. It's a matter of experimentation to find the right combination depending on your smoker, grill, and location in the country! The most common woods for smoking ribs are hickory, oak, apple, and maple.

Prepare the ribs by removing the silverskin from the bone side and rubbing them with your favorite rib rub. It should take about six hours at 200° F. or five hours at 225° F. to properly smoke-cook ribs. Never cook ribs higher than 250° F. All you do at that temperature is grill the ribs and the only rib that should be grilled are Country-style ribs. Always begin cooking ribs bone side down.

Place a remote-reading thermometer probe on the cooking rack about an inch or so from the ribs. This allows you to monitor the actual temperature of the heat around the meat. Don't let the temperature drop below 200° F. or climb above 250° F. If you smoke ribs too slowly they will dry out and turn into jerky. This is another frequent mistake of backyard chefs... they smoke their ribs too long and at too low of a heat.

After a couple of hours of smoking, baste the ribs. An hour later, wrap each slab in heavy-duty aluminum foil. Be careful not to punch holes in foil. The foil wrap allows the ribs to steam (a secret technique that makes for tender ribs). To tenderize the meat even more, pour ¼-cup of marinade or orange juice into the foil packet before carefully sealing the top of the foil. Double or triple wrap, if necessary, to be sure there are no holes in the envelope. Cook another two hours at 200° F. or 1½ hours if cooking at 225° F.

At the appropriate time, remove the ribs from the foil and place the slabs back on the grill to finish cooking and to firm up the ribs. About 30 minutes before serving baste the ribs with a mixture of two cups barbecue sauce, ¼-cup honey, and one tablespoon of rib rub.

Ribs can be frozen after the initial cooking and before saucing. Cool and double wrap the ribs in food film and heavy-duty aluminum foil before freezing. To reheat frozen ribs, remove them from freezer and let the ribs thaw for two hours, remove the plastic wrap and foil, re-wrap in foil, and heat in 220° F. oven for 45 minutes.

Basic Rib Recipe

2 slabs Spare ribs
1 cup white vinegar

1 gallon water

1 teaspoon kosher salt
1 teaspoon hot paprika
1 teaspoon dried oregano
1 teaspoon ground cayenne
1 teaspoon garlic powder

Rib Rub

1 teaspoon cracked black pepper
1 teaspoon dried thyme
1 teaspoon white pepper
1 teaspoon onion powder

1 (12-ounce) can beer
¼ cup vegetable oil
2 cloves garlic, chopped
2 tablespoons unsalted butter
2 Jalapeños, finely chopped

Rib Mop

½ cup cider vinegar
½ medium yellow onion, finely chopped
1 tablespoon Worcestershire sauce
2 tablespoons dry mustard

1 quart water
½ cup cider vinegar

Smoker liquid

1 large yellow onion, chopped
1 head garlic, roughly chopped

Spare ribs have an extra piece of meat on the underside of the rib called the brisket or tip that is removed prior to cooking. For competition, Spares are trimmed flat on left, angled on right and straight even on the top and bottom with the brisket strip removed.

Soak ribs in one gallon of water mixed with one cup of white vinegar for 20 minutes. Drain and pat dry. Score or remove silverskin and liberally apply rub on both surfaces. Wrap in food film and refrigerate at least four hours or overnight. Remove from refrigerator and bring to room temperature.

Combine mop ingredients in medium saucepan and bring to boil, reduce heat, and simmer 10 minutes.

Prepare smoker. Soak two cups of hickory chips in water for an hour. If using a Weber-style kettle, start 12 briquettes in charcoal chimney. When coals turn gray, place them on one side of kettle. Place a disposable aluminum pan on opposite side and add smoker liquid. Add a handful of drained chips to briquettes. Place ribs on cooking grid, bone side down. Cover grill and maintain temperature of 185° F. to 200° F. Add additional briquettes and wood chips as needed. Cook ribs five to six hours, turning every hour and basting with mop.

After five hours of smoking, wrap ribs in double sheets of heavy-duty aluminum foil, add mop, tightly seal, and return to grill for another two hours, adding additional briquettes as needed to keep temperature at 200° F.

About 30 minutes before serving, remove foil from ribs and return ribs to the grill. Paint ribs with sauce or serve ribs dry with table sauce on the side.

Rib Table Sauce

½ stick (4 tablespoons) unsalted butter
½ medium yellow onion, finely chopped
½ cup dark brown sugar, firmly packed
½ teaspoon ground cayenne pepper
2 tablespoons steak sauce
½ tablespoon cayenne pepper sauce
2 tablespoons orange juice
¼ cup straight Bourbon whiskey
½ tablespoon crushed red pepper flakes
½ teaspoon ground cloves
3 tablespoons dark molasses
1 tablespoon lemon juice
¾ cup cider vinegar

¾ cup ketchup
½ tablespoon Worcestershire sauce
½ cup chili sauce
½ tablespoon crushed garlic
1½ teaspoon dry mustard
1 teaspoon grated orange peel
1 teaspoon Colgin Liquid Smoke®
1 tablespoon soy sauce
1 teaspoon chili powder
2 tablespoons clover honey
1 teaspoon celery seed
½ teaspoon ground cumin
1 tablespoon prepared horseradish

In a medium saucepan, melt butter and cook onion until clear, about five minutes. Add remaining ingredients and cook over low heat about 30 minutes until thickened. Remove from heat and add horseradish.

Chinese Spare Ribs

2 pounds Spare ribs
1½ cups water
4 teaspoons Hoisin sauce

1 cup soy sauce
½ cup granulated sugar
4 teaspoons minced garlic

Mix all the ingredients, except ribs, together in a bowl. Add ribs, cover, and refrigerate for six hours to overnight. Cook spare ribs using indirect heat, about 30 minutes per side.

Winter Ribs

2 slabs Spare ribs

Rib Rub

1 cup dark brown sugar, firmly packed
½ teaspoon black pepper
½ teaspoon Old Bay® seasoning
½ teaspoon dried thyme
1 tablespoon chili powder

2 tablespoons kosher salt
½ teaspoon ground cayenne pepper
½ teaspoon Ancho chile powder
½ teaspoon onion powder

Braising Liquid

1 cup dry red wine
2 tablespoons Worcestershire sauce
4 cloves garlic, pressed

2 tablespoons wine vinegar
1 tablespoon clover honey
3 cups beef stock

Prepare the rub in a medium mixing bowl. If stored covered and in a dark cupboard, the rub will keep for several weeks.

Prepare the ribs. Season ribs with rub, cover with food film and refrigerate overnight. Bring ribs to room temperature and braise ribs in a 250° F. oven, covered, for three to 3½ hours or until tender. Remove from braising liquid, cut into serving size pieces, and cover with foil to keep warm until serving.

Clarksville Baby Backs

1 rack Baby Back ribs, silverskin removed
1 gallon water

½ cup white vinegar

Marinade

½ - ¾ cup Tennessee Gourmet™
   Apple & Spice Sauce

Spice Rub

2 teaspoons dark brown sugar
2 teaspoons sweet paprika
1½ teaspoons white pepper
1½ teaspoons kosher salt

2 teaspoons cracked black pepper
1 teaspoon chili powder
1½ teaspoons ground cayenne pepper
1 teaspoon garlic power

What's the difference between a rack and slab of ribs? A slab has 12 or more ribs while a rack is a trimmed slab usually with eight ribs. Although this recipe calls for Baby Backs, which come from the loin section of a young hog, Spare ribs may also be used although the cooking time will vary.

Mix water and vinegar. Add ribs and soak 20 minutes. Drain well and pat dry. Place ribs on a sheet of heavy-duty aluminum foil, meat side up, and brush with gourmet sauce. Seal and refrigerate overnight.

Remove from refrigerator and bring to room temperature. Dust with spice rub and indirectly grill four to five hours until tender. Cut ribs into serving-size pieces.

Coconut Barbecue Ribs

4 pounds Baby Back ribs	1 cup coconut milk
½ cup chopped fresh cilantro	½ cup light brown sugar, firmly packed
¼ cup chopped shallots	¼ cup soy sauce
3 tablespoons chopped garlic	2 tablespoons grated ginger
2 stalks lemongrass, chopped	1 teaspoon kosher salt

If fresh lemongrass is unavailable, substitute the grated peel of one lemon.

Place ribs on rack in Dutch oven. Add water to just below rack and bring to simmer. Cover and steam ribs 20 minutes. Remove ribs and cool. Combine cilantro, shallots, garlic, lemongrass, coconut milk, brown sugar, soy sauce, ginger, and salt in food processor and pulse until smooth. Transfer marinade to baking dish, add ribs, and turn to coat. Cover and refrigerate overnight.

Prepare barbecue to medium-high heat. Remove ribs from marinade, reserving marinade. Grill ribs until golden brown, about eight to 10 minutes, turning occasionally, and basting with reheated marinade. Simmer remaining marinade five minutes and serve with ribs.

Ribs 'n' Beer

1 (3½-pound) rack Spare ribs	1 teaspoon ground cumin
1 quart beer	2 teaspoons crushed red pepper flakes
2 cups dark brown sugar, firmly packed	1 tablespoon chili powder
1 cup cider vinegar	1 teaspoon dry mustard

Combine beer, sugar, vinegar, and spices in a large saucepan. Bring to a boil, remove from heat, and cool. Place ribs in a large shallow non-aluminum roasting pan. Pour marinade over ribs.

Turn ribs several times while they marinate for about 24 hours in refrigerator. Drain ribs, reserving marinade. Arrange ribs on grill and smoke five to six hours until meat is tender, basting with reheated marinade every 30 minutes.

Asian Glazed Boneless Ribs

2 pounds Country-style pork ribs

Glaze

½ cup Hoisin sauce

2 tablespoons soy sauce

2 tablespoons sesame oil

1 clove garlic, minced

¼ cup pineapple juice

2 tablespoons rice wine vinegar

½ teaspoon minced fresh ginger

Preheat grill. Arrange ribs on a microwave-safe dish. Cover with waxed paper. Microwave on medium for six to eight minutes or until outer edges begin to cook and pork is warm, turning once during cooking.

Meanwhile, in small bowl, combine all glaze ingredients and blend well.

Place ribs on grill over medium heat. Brush with glaze; cook 10 minutes. Reduce heat to medium-low by closing vents. Cook an additional 10 to 15 minutes or until tender and no longer pink, turning frequently and basting with glaze. Bring any remaining glaze to a simmer; serve with ribs.

Slow-Cooked Barbecue Spare Ribs

1 (4-pound) rack Spare ribs

¾ cup ketchup

½ cup cider vinegar

2 tablespoons cayenne pepper sauce

1 medium yellow onion, grated

3 garlic cloves, minced

1 tablespoon Worcestershire sauce

Combine the ketchup, vinegar, pepper sauce, onion, garlic, and Worcestershire sauce in a mixing bowl and stir until blended. Pour half of the sauce into a glass baking dish large enough to hold the ribs in a single layer. Place the ribs meat side down into the sauce. Pour remaining sauce over ribs; cover and refrigerate for 12 to 24 hours. Heat a charcoal grill until the coals are thickly covered with ash. If using a gas-fired grill, preheat for 10 minutes with the lid closed. Place the ribs on a rack set at least six inches from the fire. Grill over medium coals for 15 minutes. Turn and baste with sauce. Ribs should have browned slightly. Cook for another 15 minutes, baste, and turn again. Grill for 30 to 45 minutes longer, turning and basting with reheated marinade, every 15 minutes.

Beer-Braised Ribs

8 pounds Spare ribs

Rib Rub

2 tablespoons sweet paprika

1 tablespoon Old Bay® seasoning

1½ teaspoons chili powder

1½ teaspoons granulated sugar

1½ teaspoons black pepper

¾ teaspoon garlic powder

¾ teaspoon onion powder

Mopping Liquid

1 tablespoon crushed red pepper flakes

4 (12-ounce) cans beer

2½ cups dark brown sugar, firmly packed

1½ cups cider vinegar

1½ tablespoons chili powder

1½ tablespoons ground cumin

1 tablespoon dry mustard

1 teaspoon kosher salt

3 bay leaves

Sauce

4 tablespoons unsalted butter

1 medium yellow onion, finely chopped

1½ cups cider vinegar

1½ cups ketchup

1 cup dark brown sugar, firmly packed

1 tablespoon Worcestershire sauce

1 teaspoon Bellycheer® Jalapeño
Pepper Sauce

1 Chipotle pepper, finely chopped

Cut Spare ribs into four-rib sections. Score or remove the silverskin. Marinate ribs in a solution of one quart of water and one cup of white vinegar for 30 minutes. Rinse ribs and dry well.

Rub ribs with rub spices, cover with food film, and refrigerate four to six hours. Remove from refrigerator and bring ribs to room temperature.

Add mop ingredients to a large stockpot and bring to rolling boil. Reduce heat and add ribs. Simmer for 30 minutes. Remove ribs, strain the liquid, and refrigerate the liquid and ribs. After cooling, skim any fat from the surface of the liquid. Return liquid to stove and bring to boil. Simmer until reduced by one-half, about an hour.

Prepare the sauce: In a medium saucepan over medium heat, sweat the onions in butter until translucent. Add remaining ingredients, reduce heat, and simmer until reduced by one-third, about 30 to 45 minutes.

Prepare grill for medium-low indirect cooking (225° F. to 250° F.). Cook ribs, basting frequently with mop, until well glazed, about an hour, turn, and repeat on second side. Heat barbecue sauce and serve on side.

Florida Barbecued Ribs

5 pounds Spare ribs

Sauce

1 cup (2 sticks) unsalted butter

1 cup ketchup

6 limes or lemons, juiced

1 tablespoon Worcestershire sauce

½ cup cider vinegar

1 teaspoon kosher salt

1 teaspoon cayenne pepper sauce

¼ cup prepared horseradish

Prepare sauce: In a medium saucepan slowly melt butter. Add ketchup, lime or lemon juice, Worcestershire sauce, vinegar, salt, and pepper sauce. Simmer, uncovered, 20 to 25 minutes. Remove from heat and add horseradish.

Place ribs about six inches above hot coals. Lightly brush with sauce and brown on one side. Turn, brush again with sauce, and brown the other side. Continue turning and basting every 10 minutes until ribs are done, about an hour. Cut into three-rib sections and serve with any remaining sauce.

Sweet-Sour Barbecued Ribs

6 pounds Baby Back ribs

¾ cup water

2 tablespoons Worcestershire sauce

1 small yellow onion, finely chopped

½ teaspoon ground black pepper

1¼ cups ketchup

¼ cup clover honey

4 teaspoons fresh lemon juice

½ teaspoon kosher salt

Mix all ingredients except ribs and cook over medium heat for 10 minutes, stirring occasionally. Prepare grill for direct cooking and cook ribs for one hour over medium-hot coals, turning occasionally. Brush ribs with sauce. Turn and cook for 20 minutes or longer until done.

Memphis-Style Barbecue Ribs

1 (3½- to 4-pound) rack Spare ribs
1 tablespoon Old Bay® seasoning
1½ teaspoons dark brown sugar
¾ teaspoon garlic powder
2 tablespoons sweet paprika
1½ teaspoons chili powder

1½ teaspoons black pepper
½ teaspoon kosher salt
¾ teaspoon onion powder
1 tablespoon white vinegar
4 cups hickory chips

Although traditionalists would cringe at oven-smoked ribs, this recipe allows for good ribs even when the weather is prohibitive as is often the case in the northern parts of the country. Be sure your kitchen is well ventilated.

Mix the Old Bay® seasoning, sugar, garlic powder, paprika, chili powder, black pepper, salt, and onion powder in a bowl. Rub half the mixture all over the Spare ribs. Reserve the other half of the dry rub mix.

Heat the oven to 215° F. While oven is warming, soak wood chips in cold water for about 20 minutes. Remove the chips from water, drain well, and spread them evenly in the base of the smoker. Place the smoker, uncovered, on top of two stove top burners set at medium-high heat. Let the wood chips smoke for about three minutes. Then place the slab of ribs on the smoker tray, place the tray over the wood chips, and cover the smoker tightly with its lid. Turn heat down to medium and leave the smoker on the burners for five minutes. Then transfer smoker to oven placing it on the lowest rack. After the ribs have been in the oven for 1½ hours, remove the smoker and once again place it over two burners set at medium heat for five minutes. Return smoker to oven. After the ribs have been in the oven for another hour, remove the smoker from the oven. Carefully lift up the tray holding the ribs and pour off the liquid that has accumulated in the tray. Reserve the liquid. Return tray with ribs to middle portion of oven and cook for another hour. While ribs are cooking, de-grease the reserved cooking liquid and measure two tablespoons of it into a bowl. Add the vinegar and blend well. Remove ribs from oven and brush the top side with the cooking liquid-vinegar mixture. Sprinkle the dry rub mix evenly over the top side of the ribs. Cover and return to smoker. Cook another hour. Remove ribs from oven. Let stand 10 minutes. Carve into individual ribs and serve.

Barbecue Short Ribs

3 pounds beef Short ribs
1 tablespoon dark brown sugar
¼ cup cider vinegar
2 cups chicken stock
2 cups water
¼ cup ketchup

2 tablespoons tomato paste
1 tablespoon dry mustard
1 teaspoon Worcestershire sauce
¼ teaspoon ground cloves
1 teaspoon chili powder
¼ teaspoon ground cayenne pepper

The day before grilling the ribs, put the sugar and vinegar in a pot large enough to hold the ribs and place over medium heat on top of the stove. Cook until the vinegar reduces and forms into a syrup with the sugar, about eight minutes. Add the stock, water, ketchup, tomato paste, mustard, Worcestershire sauce, cloves, chili powder, and cayenne pepper and bring to a boil. Add the ribs and cook 20 minutes. Remove from heat, remove the ribs from the liquid, wrap in foil, and refrigerate. Cook the liquid over medium heat until it coats the back of a spoon. Remove from heat and reserve. The next day, grill ribs over indirect heat about 30 to 40 minutes, turning and basting with reheat sauce every 10 minutes.

Oriental Short Rib Barbecue

4 pounds beef Short ribs
½ cup thinly sliced green onions
1 cup soy sauce
2½ tablespoons brown sugar
1½ tablespoons sesame seeds
1 cup water

¼ cup dark sesame oil
1 tablespoon minced garlic
1 tablespoon grated fresh ginger
½ teaspoon ground cayenne pepper
¼ teaspoon crushed red pepper flakes

Combine green onions, soy sauce, brown sugar, sesame seeds, water, sesame oil, garlic, ginger, cayenne pepper, and crushed red pepper flakes. Place short ribs in a food-safe plastic bag; add marinade and turn to coat. Marinate in refrigerator four to six hours (or overnight), turning occasionally. Remove ribs from marinade; reserve marinade. Grill ribs over medium coals, covered, 10 to 12 minutes, turning once. Brush with reheated marinade before serving.

Michelle's Braised Ribs

6 pounds Baby Back ribs

Braising Sauce

1 large yellow onion, minced	1 teaspoon cracked black pepper
1 medium carrot, finely minced	1½ teaspoons kosher salt
1 tablespoon tomato paste	4 cups beef stock
1 celery stalk, finely sliced	3 bay leaves
1 tablespoon minced garlic	1 spring fresh thyme

Rib Sauce

1 tablespoon dark brown sugar	1 teaspoon Worcestershire sauce
¼ cup cider vinegar	¼ teaspoon ground cloves
Braising liquid from ribs	1 teaspoon chili powder
2 tablespoons ketchup	¼ teaspoon ground cayenne pepper
1 tablespoon dry mustard	

Braising Sauce: Preheat oven to 350° F. Mix onion, carrot, tomato paste, celery, and garlic together and place in a roasting pan large enough to hold the ribs in a single layer. Lay the ribs on top and season with salt and pepper. Add stock, bay leaves, and thyme. Cover and roast for an hour. Remove from oven; remove the ribs and set them aside to cool. Strain the braising liquid and discard the vegetables.

In a medium saucepan over medium heat, combine the sugar and vinegar. Cook until the vinegar reduces and forms a syrup, about eight minutes. Add the rib braising liquid then the ketchup, mustard, Worcestershire sauce, cloves, chili powder, and cayenne pepper. Cook and reduce the liquid until it has a sauce-like consistency. Remove from the heat and set aside.

Prepare grill for indirect cooking. Add two cups pre-soaked and drained hickory chips. Place the ribs on the grill so they are not directly over the coals and cook for 30 minutes, turning and basting with rib sauce every 10 minutes.

East Carolina Ribs

6 pounds Baby Back ribs

	Rub
2 tablespoons kosher salt	2 tablespoons granulated sugar
2 tablespoons dark brown sugar	2 tablespoons ground cumin
2 tablespoons chili powder	2 tablespoons black pepper
4 tablespoons sweet paprika	
	Table Sauce
1 cup white vinegar	1 cup cider vinegar
1 tablespoon crushed red pepper flakes	1 tablespoon Bellycheer® Jalapeño
2 tablespoons chili powder	Pepper Sauce
½ teaspoon black pepper	

Rub: Mix all ingredients in small bowl.

Table Sauce: Mix all ingredients together and let stand for an hour to blend flavors.

Ribs: Rub dry rub mixture over all sides of ribs and smoke in 225° F. smoker for 4½ to five hours. Remove from smoker, baste with table sauce, and finish on medium-high grill until crispy.

Barbecued Pork Ribs with Snappy Glaze

3 pounds Baby Back ribs	¼ teaspoon black pepper
1 teaspoon ground ginger	1 teaspoon kosher salt
1 teaspoon ground coriander	½ teaspoon sweet paprika
	Glaze
½ cup Tennessee Gourmet™	1 tablespoon lemon juice
Snappy Pepper Jelly	1 tablespoon Creole mustard
3 tablespoons orange juice	Orange slices for garnish

Combine spices and rub onto the meaty side of the ribs. Cover ribs and refrigerate for two hours. Remove ribs from refrigerator and bring to room temperature. An hour or so before serving, start cooking ribs five to six inches from medium hot coals turning occasionally. Pork ribs will take 60 to 70 minutes to cook depending on the thickness. Heat the pepper jelly, orange juice, and lemon juice with the mustard. Brush ribs frequently with the glaze during the last 15 minutes of cooking.

Knoxville Country Ribs

3 pounds Country-style ribs
2 yellow onions, chopped

Water

Marinade

½ - ¾ cup Tennessee Gourmet™
  Apple & Spice Sauce

Country-style ribs are actually not ribs, but chops cut from the loin's blade end behind the shoulder. Although Country-style ribs do have a lot of fat, they are the meatiest of all ribs.

Place ribs in large casserole dish, add onion, and cover with water. Cover with heavy-duty aluminum foil and bake in preheated 350° F. oven for 1½ to two hours until tender. Remove casserole from oven and carefully remove foil. Drain. Cover ribs with Tennessee Gourmet™ Apple & Spice Sauce. Allow to cool. Cover and refrigerate at least two hours or overnight.

Remove ribs from refrigerator and bring to room temperature. Lift ribs from marinade, keeping some sauce on each rib. Place ribs in clean casserole dish and re-heat in a pre-heated 300° F. oven for 30 minutes or indirectly grill on heavy-duty aluminum foil 30 to 45 minutes (ribs will stick if cooked directly on the cooking grate). Allow ribs to rest five to 10 minutes before serving.

Heat additional Tennessee Gourmet™ sauce and serve with ribs.

Two racks of Baby Backs ready for smoking

Beef kabobs ready for the grill (recipe page 103)

Pork chops brining before smoking (recipe page 138)

Seafood

Basic Seafood Instructions

Generally, saltwater fish have few thick bones while freshwater fish have many tiny bones.

Fish fillets and steaks should have a fresh aroma (they shouldn't smell "fishy") and a firm, moist feel. Fillets are a boneless, longitudinal cut from the sides of a fish. Fish steaks are cross-cut from dressed fish, are usually ½- to one-inch thick, and often contain a section of the back-bone.

Clean fish immediately after catching and refrigerate as soon as possible. Use fresh fish within a day.

Fish can be baked, broiled, fried, grilled, poached, and steamed. Generally, cook fish for 10 minutes per inch of thickness. When fully cooked, the fish will be opaque with milky white juice. Properly cooked, fish will read 145° F. internal temperature.

Grilling Fish: Marinate and rub with seasonings. Grill six to eight inches from medium heat coals 15 to 25 minutes, turning once. If using a gas-fired grill, 10 minutes at medium heat per inch of thickness is almost perfect timing. When fish begins to flake with a fork, it's done.

Avoid over-handling fish during grilling. Cooked fish will break apart easily. Turn only once.

Another way to cook fish is in foil packets although this method doesn't allow for smoking. To enhance the flavor, add a splash of white wine and lemon juice to the packets.

To avoid having shrimp fall through the grill grate, use skewers or a fish tray. Fish often falls apart or sticks to the grill. Use a hinged wire basket. Lightly coat the basket with oil to prevent sticking, insert the fish, and cook.

If you don't have a fish basket, use heavy-duty aluminum foil lightly coated with oil and placed on the grill grate.

Confused About Shellfish?

Shrimp are sold and sized by the number per pound. Colossal shrimp (U-8) are eight to the pound and weigh about two ounces. Jumbo shrimp (U-12 and U-15) weigh 1⅓ and one ounce, respectively. Extra Large shrimp (U-16/20) also weigh about one ounce. Large shrimp come in three ranges, 21/25 (⅔-ounce), 26/30 (⅔-ounce), and 31/40 (½-ounce). Medium shrimp (41/50) weigh about ¼-ounce.

Sea scallops are usually 20/30 count meaning a pound will contain 20 to 30 scallops. The average serving is five to six sea scallops (about three ounces) per person. Bay scallops, which are much smaller, average 60 to 100 per pound and the average three-ounce serving is 15 scallops.

Hard-shell clams are called different names depending on size. Littlenecks, the smallest and usually about two inches in diameter, average 10 to 12 clams per pound; top necks, six to eight per pound; cherrystones, three to five per pound; and chowders, one to two per pound. Littlenecks and top necks are often served raw on the half shell. Chowders are chopped and used for clam chowder, clam cakes, or clam fritters. One pound of hard-shell clams (also called by their Indian name, quahog, on the East Coast) yields about four ounces of meat while a pound of soft-shell clams (called steamers or longneck clams in New England) will yield about eight ounces of meat. Popular West Coast varieties of soft-shell clam are the razor clam and geoduck clam.

Shellfish is very perishable and should be stored under refrigeration and used within two days. Do not soak shellfish in fresh water. It will kill them. Shucked clams may be stored, refrigerated, for four days.

Confused About Fish?

Sometimes the same fish is called by different names depending on what part of the country you're in.

For example, mahi-mahi is the Hawaiian name for dolphin fish, which is not the same as Flipper, a mammal that is also called a dolphin. The same dolphin fish caught in South American waters is called Dorado but sold as mahi-mahi. Another bewildering name is scrod. Scrod is a young cod or haddock weighing less than 2½ pounds. The same name, scrod, goes to either species.

Bass is also a general term for several freshwater and saltwater fish. True bass include the groupers, black sea bass, and striped bass, all saltwater fish. Other fish commonly called bass are the largemouth, rock, and smallmouth bass, all of which are in the sunfish family. When in doubt, it's always best to ask your fishmonger what you're really buying and get his or her recommendations for cooking.

Aussie Shrimp on the Barbie with Orange Ginger Sauce

12 jumbo shrimp (U-12 size)
1 cup orange juice
1 teaspoon grated orange peel
1 teaspoon grated fresh ginger

¼ cup unsalted butter
2 tablespoons dry sherry
2 green onions, minced

Shell and devein the shrimp. Soak a dozen long wooden skewers in water for 30 minutes. Then push skewers through shrimp, lengthwise, from head to tail with only one shrimp to a skewer. Combine all ingredients, except shrimp, in saucepan and cook over medium heat, stirring, until butter melts completely. Dip skewered shrimp in the orange sauce and position on oiled grill rack about four inches above the coals. Baste liberally with sauce and grill for three minutes. Turn the shrimp over and baste again, cooking for another three minutes. Smaller shrimp will be done at this point, but continue basting and turning larger shrimp until they are pink and cooked through. Remove from heat immediately when done, as they will get tough if overcooked. Reheat any remaining sauce and use as a dipping sauce.

Grilled Shrimp

2 pounds large shrimp (U-21)
¼ cup olive oil
¼ cup tomato sauce
2 tablespoons red wine vinegar

2 tablespoons chopped basil
1 tablespoon minced garlic
½ teaspoon kosher salt
½ teaspoon cayenne pepper

Peel and devein the shrimp. In a bowl stir together the oil, tomato sauce, vinegar, basil, minced garlic, salt, and cayenne pepper. Add the shrimp and toss to coat evenly. Cover and refrigerate for two hours, stirring occasionally. Put shrimp on skewers and cook on medium-hot grill for about three minutes per side, basting with reheated marinade.

Shrimp and Biscuits

2 pounds medium shrimp	3 lemons, peeled and quartered
2 tablespoons Cajun spice (Page 44)	2 cups water
1 teaspoon cracked black pepper	½ cup Worcestershire sauce
2 tablespoons olive oil	¼ cup dry white wine
½ tablespoon chopped onion	¼ teaspoon kosher salt
2 tablespoons minced garlic	2 cups heavy cream
3 bay leaves	2 tablespoons unsalted butter

Buttermilk Biscuits

1 teaspoon baking powder	1 cup all-purpose flour
¼ teaspoon kosher salt	2 tablespoons unsalted butter
⅛ teaspoon baking soda	¼ cup plus 1 teaspoon buttermilk

Peel and devein the shrimp, leaving only the tails attached. Reserve the shells; sprinkle the shrimp with one tablespoon of Cajun spice and ½-teaspoon black pepper. Refrigerate the shrimp while making the sauce base and biscuits.

Heat one tablespoon of the oil in a large pot over high heat. When the oil is hot, add the onions and garlic and cook for one minute. Add the reserved shrimp shells, the remaining tablespoon Cajun spice, the bay leaves, lemons, water, Worcestershire sauce, wine, salt, and the remaining ½-teaspoon of black pepper. Stir well and bring to a boil. Reduce the heat and simmer for 30 minutes. Remove from heat, allow to cool, and strain into a small saucepan. Place over high heat, bring to a boil, and cook until a thick, dark brown syrup forms, about 15 minutes.

Prepare the biscuits: Preheat the oven to 375° F. Line a baking sheet with parchment or waxed paper. In a bowl combine the dry ingredients and blend thoroughly. Cream in the butter until the mixture resembles coarse crumbs. Add the buttermilk a little at a time and thoroughly incorporate. Roll out the dough on a lightly floured surface to a circle about seven inches in diameter, ½-inch thick. Using a small cookie cutter or white wine glass, press out 12 one-inch rounds. Place the dough rounds on the baking sheet and bake until golden on top and brown on the bottom, about 15 minutes.

Heat the remaining one tablespoon of oil in a large skillet over high heat. When the oil is hot, add the seasoned shrimp and sauté for two minutes. Add the cream and the entire sauce base. Stir and simmer for three to five minutes. Remove the shrimp to a warm platter with tongs and whisk the butter into the sauce. When butter has melted, remove sauce from heat and drizzle over shrimp.

Charbroiled Shrimp

1 pound large shrimp (U-21)
1 cup olive oil
¼ cup chopped fresh parsley

2 cloves garlic, crushed
2 tablespoons fresh lemon juice
1 teaspoon kosher salt

Peel and devein shrimp, leaving tails attached. Combine olive oil and remaining ingredients in a baking dish; stir well; add shrimp, stirring gently; cover and marinate in refrigerator for at least two hours, stirring occasionally; remove shrimp from marinade; reserve marinade. Grill shrimp over medium hot coals three to four minutes on each side basting frequently with reheated marinade.

Indonesian Barbecued Shrimp

Dipping sauce

½ cup water
1 tablespoon lemon juice
½ teaspoon cayenne pepper sauce
1 small garlic clove, crushed

½ cup peanut butter
1 tablespoon dark brown sugar
½ teaspoon kosher salt

Shrimp

1½ pounds medium shrimp
2 tablespoons water
1 teaspoon dark brown sugar
½ teaspoon cayenne pepper sauce

2 tablespoons vegetable oil
1 tablespoon lemon juice
½ teaspoon kosher salt
2 garlic cloves, crushed

Prepare dipping sauce by mixing all ingredients until smooth. Cover until serving time. Peel and devein shrimp. Mix remaining ingredients in medium glass bowl. Add shrimp; stir to coat with marinade. Cover and refrigerate at least one hour. Remove shrimp from marinade; reserve marinade. Thread shrimp on six 15-inch metal or wooden skewers, leaving space between each. Grill shrimp about four inches from medium coals, three to five minutes per side, turning and brushing two to three times with reheated marinade, until shrimp are pink. Serve with sauce and lemon or lime wedges.

Grilled Scallops with Plum Sauce

16 large sea scallops
¼ cup plum preserves
1 tablespoon horseradish

¼ cup ketchup
2 tablespoons lime juice
¼ teaspoon black pepper

Wash scallops in cold water, dry well. Mix remaining ingredients in small bowl. Arrange scallops in a single layer in a 1½-quart casserole and spoon six tablespoons of the ketchup/plum mixture over scallops. Cover and refrigerate for 30 minutes.

Remove scallops from marinade, reserving marinade. Grill scallops over hot coals four to six minutes per side. Simmer reserved marinade for five minutes. When scallops are cooked, drizzle with reheated marinade. Garnish with lemon and lime slices.

Grilled Chili-Dijon Shrimp

1½ pounds medium shrimp
3 slices bacon, chopped
½ pound unsalted butter
1½ teaspoons chili powder
1 teaspoon black pepper

3 cloves garlic, crushed
2 tablespoons Dijon-style mustard
¼ teaspoon dried basil
½ teaspoon dried oregano
2 tablespoons Old Bay® seasoning

Shell and devein shrimp leaving tails attached. Preheat grill to medium heat (375° F.). In a medium sauté pan, cook bacon until clear, add butter and remaining ingredients except shrimp. Simmer for five minutes and cool. Place shrimp in casserole dish and pour cooled sauce over shrimp. Stir once to coat and refrigerate 30 minutes. Remove shrimp from marinade, drain, reserving marinade. Boil marinade five minutes and use as baste. Place shrimp on metal or pre-soaked wooden skewers. Grill, basting with re-heated marinade, about three minutes per side until opaque.

Grilled Swordfish with Cilantro-Lime Sauce

1 (1½-pound) Swordfish steak, 1-inch thick

Marinade

¼ cup dry white wine
1 tablespoon olive oil
1 tablespoon chopped fresh cilantro

2 tablespoons lime juice
1 tablespoon Tamari soy sauce

Rinse fish in cold water. In a gallon-size resealable plastic bag, combine the marinade ingredients. Add fish and marinate, refrigerated, for an hour.

Preheat grill to medium heat (375° F.). Spray cooking grate with nonstick cooking spray and place about five inches from the heat. Drain marinade into small saucepan and bring to boil. Simmer five minutes. Grill fish five to six minutes per side. Pour marinade over fish and serve.

Grilled Tennessee Mahi-Mahi

4 (6- to 7-ounce) mahi-mahi fillets
½ teaspoon kosher salt
½ teaspoon black pepper
¼ cup Tennessee Gourmet™
    Salad Dressing Plus

½ tablespoon minced ginger
½ tablespoon minced garlic

Tuna steaks, Chilean Sea Bass, or any firm white fish may be substituted for the mahi-mahi, if desired.

Prepare the mahi-mahi; season the fish with salt and pepper. Combine Tennessee Gourmet™ Salad Dressing Plus with the ginger and garlic and rub evenly over the fillets.

Preheat a grill to a high temperature to keep fillets from sticking. Cook the fish on the grill for approximately four to five minutes per side or to an internal temperature of 145° F.

Chile-Seared Shrimp

1 pound large shrimp (U-21)

Marinade

¼ teaspoon kosher salt
½ teaspoon black pepper
1½ teaspoons Cajun spice, divided
¼ cup minced garlic

¼ cup extra virgin olive oil
2 tablespoons Chipotle chile purée
½ cup fresh lime juice

Peel and devein shrimp leaving tails intact. Season shrimp with salt, pepper, and ¾ teaspoon of Cajun spice (Page 44). Mix garlic with olive oil, add shrimp, and marinate for 10 to 15 minutes, refrigerated. Drain shrimp, reserving marinade. Bring marinade to low boil, add Chipotle purée, remaining Cajun spice, and lime juice. Simmer five minutes.

Prepare grill to medium heat. Grill shrimp until cooked, about three to four minutes per side. Toss with marinade and serve. (Excellent with Ranch Gazpacho, Page 181)

Oysters

Lay aluminum foil on the grill or use a Sam's Smoker Fish and Kabob tray. Scrub oysters well and place on indirect grill. Smoke over alder or pecan wood for an hour at 230° F. Do not let the oysters cook dry. Serve with Tamari soy sauce, wasabi, and pickled ginger.

New Orleans Barbecue Shrimp

2 pounds U-12 or U-8 shrimp
1 cup dry white wine
1 cup bottled clam juice
1 medium lemon, sliced
1 tablespoon Old Bay® seasoning
1 teaspoon kosher salt, divided
1 teaspoon black pepper

8 tablespoons butter, divided
1 cup chopped yellow onion
2 teaspoons minced garlic
1 cup mild barbecue sauce
2 tablespoons Worcestershire sauce
1 teaspoon cayenne pepper sauce
2 tablespoons chopped chives

Not a true barbecue recipe, but a wonderful appetizer!

Peel and devein the shrimp, leaving only the tails attached, reserving shells. In a medium saucepan, add shells, wine, clam juice, sliced lemon, Old Bay®, and ½ teaspoon of kosher salt. Bring to boil over medium heat. Reduce heat and simmer, covered, for 15 minutes. Strain stock and reserve liquid.

Melt four tablespoons of butter in sauté pan over medium heat. Add onions and dash salt. Sweat onions until soft. Add garlic and cook one minute. Add shrimp stock, barbecue sauce, Worcestershire sauce, and ½ teaspoon of pepper. Bring to boil.

Add shrimp and cayenne pepper sauce. Return sauce to boil. Cover, reduce heat, and simmer three to four minutes, until shrimp turn pink. Add remaining butter. Sprinkle with chives and season with salt and cracked black pepper. Serve in bowls with crusty bread.

Jumbo Shrimp with Bacon

Get the largest fresh shrimp available (U-8 or U-12). Shell and devein; leave the tails attached. Take one slice of bacon and wrap the shrimp, securing with wooden picks. Season shrimp with barbecue sauce and a little garlic powder. Place the shrimp on side of the grill away from the fire. Smoke for 25 to 25 minutes at 200° F. to 225° F. Mop with garlic butter and serve hot.

Honey Grilled Shrimp

1 pound jumbo shrimp (U-12)
3 tablespoons soy sauce
1 tablespoon chile sauce
2 cloves garlic, pressed
2 green onions, finely chopped
2 tablespoons Asian sesame oil

5 tablespoons Sake
1½ tablespoons clover honey
¼ teaspoon five-spice powder
¾ teaspoons grated fresh ginger
1½ tablespoons sesame seeds

Peel and devein the shrimp, leaving tails attached. Rinse with cold water and reserve. In a medium mixing bowl, stir together the remaining ingredients, mixing well. Add shrimp and marinate, covered and refrigerated, at least 30 minutes or up to two hours.

Prepare grill for medium high direct cooking. Remove shrimp from marinade, strain and reserve marinade, discarding solids. Bring marinade to low boil over medium heat and simmer at least five minutes until marinade forms a thick glaze.

Grill shrimp three to four minutes per side, until cooked through, brushing with glaze frequently.

Mt. Juliet Shrimp On The Barbie

12 jumbo shrimp (U-8 or U-12 size)
2 green onions, finely chopped
1 teaspoon grated orange peel
1 teaspoon grated fresh ginger

¼ cup unsalted butter
2 tablespoons dry sherry
1 cup Tennessee Gourmet™
    Salad Dressing Plus

Shell and devein the shrimp, leaving tails attached. Combine all ingredients, except shrimp, in saucepan and cook over medium heat, stirring, until butter is completely melted. Dip shrimp in the sauce and position on oiled grill rack about four inches above hot coals. Baste liberally with sauce and grill for three minutes. Turn the shrimp over and baste again, cooking for another three minutes. Smaller shrimp will be done at this point, but continue basting and turning larger shrimp until they are pink and cooked through. Use any remaining sauce, reheated, as a dipping sauce.

Spicy Grilled Sea Scallops

10 large sea scallops
2 Chipotle peppers, finely chopped
2 tablespoons chopped cilantro
2 tablespoons lime juice
1 tablespoon honey

¼ cup Tennessee Gourmet™ Salad Dressing Plus
¼ teaspoon kosher salt
¼ teaspoon black pepper
2 tablespoons adobo sauce

Chipotle peppers in adobo sauce are available in most supermarkets. The sauce is made from ground chiles, vinegar, and herbs.

Combine Chipotle peppers, cilantro, lime, honey, Tennessee Gourmet™ Salad Dressing Plus, salt, pepper, and adobo sauce in a medium bowl. Add scallops and coat well.

Grill scallops two to three minutes per side, basting with sauce.

Grilled Maine Lobster

2 (1½-pound) Maine lobsters
8 tablespoons unsalted butter

2 tablespoons kosher salt
2 lemons

Maine lobsters, unlike their southern cousin the Spiny Lobster, have two large claws containing sweet meat. This recipe is adapted from grilling directions by Maine Lobster Direct, Portland, Maine (lobsterdirect.com).

Fill a large stockpot two-thirds full of water. Add two tablespoons kosher salt. Bring to rolling boil and add lobsters. Cook three to five minutes. Remove lobsters and cool. With a large chef's knife or kitchen shears, split the lobster into two longitudinal halves and crack the large claws. Rinse the body cavity with cold water to remove the intestinal tract, being careful not to wash out any tomalley.

Microwave the lemons for one minute to release the juices. Melt butter and add the juice of one lemon. Section the other lemon into quarters. Divide melted butter into two equal portions, reserving one for serving.

Brush the lobster meat with melted butter and pour some of the butter into the cracked claws. Over a medium-hot grill, grill the lobster halves about three inches from the coals, shell side down and with the grill cover closed, eight to 10 minutes. Don't overcook the lobsters. If overcooked, the meat will become tough.

Prosciutto-Wrapped Scallops with Tomato Concassé

1 pound sea scallops	1 tablespoon minced garlic
1 teaspoon Cajun spice (Page 44)	2 tablespoons minced shallots
½ teaspoon kosher salt, divided	¼ cup extra virgin olive oil
½ teaspoon black pepper	¼ cup dry white wine
½ pound sliced Prosciutto ham	2 tablespoons chopped basil
2 large tomatoes	

Rinse scallops and clean if necessary. Season with Cajun spice, ¼-teaspoon salt, and black pepper. Slice Prosciutto into one-inch width. Wrap Prosciutto around scallops and secure with wooden pick. Refrigerate if not using immediately.

Bring one quart of water to a rolling boil in a medium saucepan. Core tomatoes and score bottom. Plunge tomatoes into boiling water for one minute, remove, and shock in ice bath. Peel, seed, and roughly chop tomatoes.

In a medium bowl, add tomatoes, garlic, shallots, olive oil, wine, ¼-teaspoon salt, and basil. Stir well and allow flavors to incorporate at least an hour.

Prepare medium hot grill, sear scallops four minutes on one side, turn, and cook another four minutes. Remove from grill and serve with tomato-basil concassé.

Gatlinburg Grilled Shrimp Mesclun Salad

30 large shrimp, peeled	Kosher salt
½ tablespoon minced garlic	Cracked black pepper
1 tablespoon grated ginger	30 grape tomatoes
¼ cup chopped green onions	6 slices red onion
1 cup Tennessee Gourmet™	6 cups Mesclun mix
Salad Dressing Plus, divided	

This recipe serves six as a salad course. Mesclun is a mix of baby lettuces and wild greens including chervil, arugula, mizuna, mache, and endive.

Shell and devein the shrimp, leaving tails attached. Combine garlic, ginger, green onions, and ½-cup Tennessee Gourmet™ Salad Dressing Plus in a non-reactive bowl. Add shrimp and stir to cover. Marinate, refrigerated, one to two hours.

Remove shrimp from marinade, discarding marinade. Season the shrimp with salt and pepper. Grill shrimp over medium heat, about three to four minutes per side, basting with Tennessee Gourmet™ Salad Dressing Plus.

To serve, arrange one cup of Mesclun, five longitudinally sliced tomatoes, and one slice of red onion on plate, top with five shrimp and drizzle with dressing.

Waynesboro Shrimp

1 pound medium shrimp
1 gallon water
1 cup (2 sticks) margarine, divided
¼ cup minced garlic
½ cup Tennessee Gourmet™
   Salad Dressing Plus, divided

1 bag crab boil spices
   (or 2 tablespoons Old Bay® seasoning)
2 lemons, quartered
1 teaspoon cracked black pepper
¼ cup chopped fresh parsley

This recipe uses margarine, not butter, as the margarine will remain liquid while sautéing the shrimp. Although not a barbecue recipe, this is a great appetizer for outdoor eating.

Rinse shrimp under cold water. Prepare ice bath by dumping two trays of ice cubes into large mixing bowl and adding cold water, filling about three-fourths full. Make garlic sauce by melting two sticks margarine in a medium saucepan. Add minced garlic and sauté briefly. Add ¼-cup Salad Dressing Plus and keep warm over low heat.

In a large stockpot, bring water to boil. Juice lemons into water and add lemon quarters to pot. Add crab boil spices, cover, and return to a rolling boil for five minutes. Add shrimp, cover, and return to boil. Cook shrimp three minutes, remove with wire strainer and drain well. Shock shrimp in an ice bath to stop cooking. Be careful not to overcook shrimp or they will become tough and chewy.

Melt three tablespoons garlic sauce in large sauté pan over medium-high heat. Add cracked black pepper and parsley. Add about 10 well-drained shrimp and sauté two to three minutes, turning constantly, until thoroughly heated. Remove to serving plate. Cook remaining shrimp in batches and remove to individual serving plates. Drizzle with Tennessee Gourmet™ Salad Dressing Plus and pan sauce, season with salt and pepper, and serve.

Serve side container of warmed garlic sauce for dipping.

Bacon-Wrapped Scallops with Plum Sauce

12 large sea scallops	6 slices smoked bacon
½ cup plum preserves	¼ teaspoon black pepper
¼ cup Tennessee Gourmet™ Salad Dressing Plus	¼ teaspoon kosher salt
	2 long wooden skewers

Combine plum preserves and Tennessee Gourmet™ Salad Dressing Plus.

Soak two wooden skewers in water for 30 minutes. Blanch bacon in boiling water for two minutes. Remove and pat dry. Trim bacon to width of scallops.

Season scallops with salt and pepper. Wrap bacon around each scallop and place three scallops on a skewer, using the skewer to secure the bacon (leave some space between each scallop to allow for even cooking). Prepare a medium hot grill for direct cooking. Place scallop skewers on grill and baste with plum glaze. Cook three to four minutes on each side, basting after each turn.

Beale Street Coconut Shrimp

1 pound large shrimp	2 tablespoons granulated sugar
1 tablespoon hot Hungarian paprika	2 cups unsweetened shredded coconut
1 cup all-purpose flour	1 cup flat beer
1 teaspoon kosher salt	Vegetable oil for deep-frying
1 teaspoon baking powder	1 cup Tennessee Gourmet™ Apple & Spice Sauce
¼ teaspoon baking soda	

Not a barbecue dish, but a tasty appetizer for outdoor festivities. These shrimp may also be prepared in a turkey fryer.

Peel and devein shrimp, leaving tails attached. Rinse shrimp under cold water. Dry shrimp thoroughly and sprinkle with paprika. In a medium bowl, completely mix flour, salt, baking powder, and baking soda. Add sugar and ½-cup shredded coconut. Add beer and mix well. Put remaining coconut in a shallow pie plate.

Dip shrimp into batter and roll in coconut, coating well. Place on parchment paper lined sheet pan. Continue dipping and coating shrimp until all the shrimp have been prepared. Refrigerate, covered loosely with food film, for 20 minutes or up to an hour.

Fill electric skillet or turkey fryer with two inches of oil and heat to 350° F. Cook shrimp, turning frequently, in small batches, five or six minutes or until they float. Remove and drain on paper towels. Keep shrimp warm in low (200° F.) oven until all the shrimp are cooked.

Plate and serve side ramekins with ¼ cup of warmed Tennessee Gourmet™ sauce for dipping.

Marinated shrimp cooking on the grill

Grilled shrimp ready to be served

Vegetables

Aside from the rich, complex smoky flavors of meat slowly cooked in a true barbecue, probably some of the best cooking to come from a grill or smoker are garden-fresh vegetables. Adding to the distinctive grill marks that make for great presentation, grilling and smoking vegetables adds layers of flavors from the caramelizing of the sugars in the vegetables and the aromatic smoke.

Chipotle Chiles (Smoked Jalapeño Chiles)

1 pound ripe Jalapeño chiles	10 pounds lump charwood
Mesquite chips, as needed	Sprigs of fresh rosemary

Put mesquite in a container and cover with water. Mound about one-half the charwood into a kettle grill and light. Wash the chiles and cut a slit lengthwise in each one from just below the shoulder to about a half-inch from the tip. When the charwood is covered with gray ash, spread it out into an even layer leaving a drip pan in the middle of the kettle. Place some of the soaked and drained chips on the charwood. Fill the drip pan with two to three inches of water. Put the cooking grate in place, place chiles on the rack over the drip pan, and cover the kettle. Keep a 180° F. to 200° F. smoldering, smoky fire for several hours. Add charcoal, wood chips, and sprigs of fresh rosemary as needed to keep generating heat and smoke. After six or seven hours, remove the chiles from the kettle grill and finish drying in a 200° F. oven or a dehydrator.

Honey-Grilled Vegetables

12 small red potatoes, halved	1 medium eggplant, sliced into
2 medium zucchini, halved	½-inch thick rounds
lengthwise and crosswise	1 large red onion,
1 red and green bell pepper, cut	sliced into ½-inch rounds
vertically into eighths	¼ cup clover honey
3 tablespoons dry white wine	1 clove garlic, minced
½ teaspoon kosher salt	½ teaspoon black pepper
1 teaspoon dried thyme	

Cover potatoes with water and bring to a boil over high heat, reduce heat and simmer five minutes; drain. Combine the honey, wine, garlic, salt, pepper, and thyme in a non-reactive container; mix well. Place vegetables on an oiled cooking grate over hot coals. Grill 20 to 25 minutes, turning and brushing with the honey mixture every 10 minutes.

Roasted Garlic

Set grill about six inches above medium-hot coals. Roast whole garlic heads, turning frequently, 45 to 50 minutes or until tender when pierced with a knife. Press the individual cloves to squeeze out the garlic and serve with grilled meats. Use roasted garlic mixed with softened butter for garlic bread, garlic-mashed potatoes, and for basting meats. Garlic may also be smoked for one to two hours with hickory chips.

Carolina Slaw

1 head green cabbage, shredded	1 teaspoon caraway seed
3 carrots, shaved	1 tablespoon celery seed
1 cup Carolina vinegar mop	

A traditional side served in the South that goes particularly well with pulled pork.

Mix cabbage with vinegar mop (Page 58), add carrots, and seasonings. Mix well. Refrigerate at least two hours before serving to blend flavors.

Corn Boil

1 package crab boil (or seasoning below)	20 ears fresh corn
2 heads garlic	2 large yellow onions
1 lemon	2 tablespoons kosher salt
3 tablespoons Old Bay®	2 sticks unsalted butter

Crab Boil Seasoning

¼ cup pickling spices	2 tablespoons yellow mustard seeds
2 tablespoons black peppercorns	2 tablespoons crushed red pepper flakes
1 tablespoon celery seeds	2 teaspoons ground ginger
5 bay leaves, crumbled	2 teaspoons dried oregano
1 tablespoon minced chives	¼ cup kosher salt

Although not barbecue, boiled fresh corn goes well with most barbecues!

Husk corn and remove silk. Cut each ear in half. Peel and quarter onions. Cut garlic heads in half and cut lemon into quarters.

Fill a turkey fryer or large kettle about half full of water. Add crab boil spices (either one package of commercial crab boil or two tablespoons of the seasoning mixture secured with cheesecloth), onion, garlic, lemon, and salt. Bring to high boil. Add corn and cook eight to 10 minutes or until tender. Combine melted butter with Old Bay® and brush over cooked corn. (Serves 10)

Roasted Potatoes

Rub whole potatoes with herbed butter or olive oil. Sprinkle with salt and pepper. Place in smoker and smoke over hickory for 1½ to two hours at 250° F.

Roasted Onions

Select medium-size onions; do not peel. Drop onions directly into hot coals. Turn often and cook until dark brown or black all over. Remove from coals, allow to cool, and cut off the bottom end. Squirt the onion out of the burnt skin and serve.

Roasted Corn

Shuck and wash corn, pat dry. Rub generously with butter, season with salt and pepper. Wrap in foil. Cook on indirect grill for about 20 to 30 minutes, turning once. Alternatively, carefully remove silk from corn; soak corn with husk in water for one hour. Re-wrap husks around corn, secure with butcher's twine, and cook for same time. Before serving, paint with melted butter and sprinkle with Cajun spice.

Roasted Peppers

Place whole green or red sweet peppers on the grill, six to eight inches from the coals. Cook, turning often, until the skin blisters and peppers char on all sides. Remove from grill, wrap in a damp towel, and let cool. When cool, use a sharp paring knife to remove the charred skin. Discard skin, core, and seeds. Rinse quickly under cool water and pat dry. Store roasted peppers in a plastic bag or container and use in any recipe calling for peppers. Freeze the peppers only if you intend to use them in purées or soups.

Mixed Vegetables

Cut any variety you choose into large pieces and brushed with olive oil. Sprinkled with herbs and freshly cracked black pepper. Grill for about five to 10 minutes until tender.

New England Coleslaw

1 head green cabbage, shredded	½ teaspoon kosher salt
1½ cups mayonnaise	½ teaspoon cracked black pepper
3 carrots, shaved	1 tablespoon granulated sugar
½ cup chopped red onion	1 tablespoon celery seed
½ cup white vinegar	

Mix cabbage with mayonnaise, add carrots, onion, vinegar, and seasonings. Mix well. Cover and refrigerate at least two hours before serving to blend flavors.

Oriental Slaw

2½ cups shredded red cabbage
6 green onions, chopped
1 cup shredded carrots
2½ cups shredded broccoli stalks

4 tablespoons coleslaw dressing
½ cup Tennessee Gourmet™
  Salad Dressing Plus
4 tablespoons slivered almonds

In a large mixing bowl, combine cabbage, green onions, carrots, and broccoli. Add coleslaw dressing and Tennessee Gourmet™ Salad Dressing Plus. Blend well. Cover and refrigerate at least an hour for flavors to incorporate. Remove from refrigerator, garnish with almonds, and serve.

Roasted Potato Planks

2 medium baking potatoes
3 tablespoons olive oil
2 cloves garlic, minced

½ teaspoon kosher salt
½ teaspoon black peppercorns
½ teaspoon garlic powder

Quarter the potatoes. Heat grill to 400° F. In large bowl, combine potatoes, oil, and garlic; toss to coat. Season potatoes with salt, pepper, and garlic powder. Indirectly grill 40 to 45 minutes or until tender and browned, turning potatoes after 25 minutes. Serve with sour cream and chopped green onions. (Serves two)

Snappy Green Beans & Peppers

1 pound green string beans
1 large red or green bell pepper
1 teaspoon minced garlic
3 tablespoons Tennessee
  Gourmet™ Pepper Jelly

1 shallot, finely chopped
3 tablespoons lemon juice
¼ teaspoon kosher salt
½ teaspoon black pepper
1 teaspoon caraway seeds

Snap ends off the beans and slice peppers into thin julienne. In a medium saucepan of heavily salted boiling water, blanch beans three minutes, drain, and shock in ice bath to set color and stop cooking.

Drain beans. In a large mixing bowl combine beans and remaining ingredients and marinate at least an hour. Remove from marinade, reserving marinade.

Using the grill's side burner or your stove top, cook the green beans and pepper slices in a medium sauté pan three to four minutes or until crisp-tender. Toss with reserved marinade, heat to low simmer and serve immediately.

Julienned Vegetables

½ tablespoon Asian sesame oil
1 teaspoon minced garlic
1 teaspoon minced ginger
1 cup julienned pea pods
1 cup sliced shitake mushrooms
½ cup julienned leeks
1 cup julienned carrots

½ teaspoon kosher salt
½ teaspoon ground black pepper
¼ cup Tennessee Gourmet™
   Salad Dressing Plus
1 tablespoon minced cilantro
1 teaspoon black sesame seeds

Using the grill's side burner, heat a large sauté pan over medium heat and add the sesame oil. When the oil is hot, add the garlic and ginger. Cook briefly. Add all the julienned vegetables, salt, and pepper and cook for two minutes, stirring often. Once the vegetables begin to soften, add Tennessee Gourmet™ Salad Dressing Plus and the cilantro. Garnish with sesame seeds and serve immediately. (Serves four)

Kingsport Acorn Squash

2 Acorn squash
2 teaspoons honey
½ teaspoon black pepper
4 tablespoons Tennessee
   Gourmet™ Pepper Jelly

2 tablespoons unsalted butter
½ teaspoon kosher salt
1 clove garlic, minced

Cut squash in half length-wise. Remove seeds. Pierce flesh, without going through skin, in several areas. Mix remaining ingredients in small bowl.

Over a medium high grill, grill the squash, flesh side down. Cook until grill marks show, about 10 minutes, rotate 90 degrees, and grill another 10 minutes. Turn the squash over and fill with the jelly mixture. Grill, covered, for 45 minutes to an hour until fork tender.

Ranch Gazpacho

Vegetables

1½ cucumbers, peeled & finely chopped

1 teaspoon minced fresh garlic

1 red bell pepper, finely chopped

1 green bell pepper, finely chopped

½ cup finely chopped yellow onion

½ cup finely chopped red onion

4 large tomatoes, finely chopped

3 green onions, finely chopped

Liquids

2 cups V-8® juice

1½ cups Spicy V-8® juice

¾ teaspoon Worcestershire sauce

1 teaspoon cayenne pepper sauce

¼ cup lemon juice

¼ cup extra virgin olive oil

1 tablespoon red wine vinegar

Seasonings

1 teaspoon black pepper

¼ teaspoon ground Chipotle chile

½ teaspoon celery salt

1 tablespoon granulated sugar

½ teaspoon kosher salt

1 tablespoon kosher salt

While another non-barbecue recipe, a favorite summertime cold soup that goes great with outdoors gatherings.

In a medium colander, add prepared cucumbers and sprinkle with one tablespoon of kosher salt. Mix well and let cucumbers drain 15 minutes, stirring occasionally. Rinse well and reserve.

In a large mixing bowl, combine liquids and seasonings; add vegetables, including cucumber. Stir to incorporate. Cover with food film and refrigerate four to six hours or overnight. Garnish with toasted croutons and chopped green onions tops. (Serve with Seared Chile Shrimp, Page 169.)

Guide For Grilling Vegetables

Vegetable	Preparation	Cooking Time	Comments
Asparagus	Snap off tough ends	Eight minutes, turning once	Marinate in olive oil, garlic, and pepper
Bell Peppers	Grill whole or quartered	Char skin by grilling on high for 15 to 20 minutes. If grilling quarters, cook for six to eight minutes	If whole, cool in paper bag. Peel and slice.
Carrots	Peel large carrots and slice on bias	20 to 30 minutes	Cook slowly
Mushrooms (Portabello)	Remove stems and wipe caps	10 to 12 minutes	Marinate for two hours before cooking. Portabello mushrooms are great on the grill.
Onion (Yellow or red)	Cut into quarters or thick slices	35 to 40 minutes (quartered); 12 to 15 minutes if sliced	
Potato (Baker)	Wash and season skin with salt and pepper	60 to 70 minutes	Use indirect heat
Squash (Acorn)	Slice in half lengthwise, remove seeds	45 to 60 minutes	Fill cavity with one tablespoon butter and one tablespoon dark brown sugar
Squash (Yellow)	Slice in half lengthwise	8 to 10 minutes	Brush with olive oil and season with black pepper
Tomatoes	Cut in half	6 to 8 minutes	Season with olive oil, black pepper, and fresh basil
Yams (Sweet Potatoes)	Peel and slice Lengthwise or leave whole	If sliced, grill about 10 minutes per side. If whole, cook for 60 to 90 minutes using indirect heat	

Marinated in olive oil and herbs, these grilled asparagus goes well with any meal or in a salad

Artichokes take on a unique flavor when smoked or grilled

Roasting or smoking corn helps caramelize the sugars giving an even sweeter taste

Index

Lump Hardwood

Cowboy Charcoal
Brentwood, TN 37204
(800) 775-4060
cowboycharcoal.com

Hasty-Bake
Tulsa, OK 74147
(800) 426-6836
hastybake.com

Smoking Pellets

BBQr's Delight, Inc.
Pine Bluff, AR 71611
(870) 535-2247
bbqrsdelight.com

Ceramic Grill Tiles

Distinctive Culinary
Concepts
Avon, OH 44011
(440) 934-9444
thenoflaresquare.com

Bullet Smokers

Masterbuilt Mfg., Inc.
Columbus, GA 31906
(800) 489-1581
masterbuilt.com

Publications

National Barbecue News
Douglas, GA 31354
(800) 385-0002
barbecuenews.com

Custom Smokers

BBQ Pits by Klose
Houston, TX 77018
(800) 487-7487
bbqpits.com

Ken's Custom BBQ Pits
Houston, TX 77018
(713) 956-8443
kenscustombbqpits.com

Smoker Trays

Sam's Smoker Pro
Hartford, WI 53027
(262) 673-0677
samssmoker.com

Spices & Herbs

Suttons Bay Trading Co.
Ft. Wayne, IN 46808
(888) 747-7423
suttonsbaytrading.com

Gourmet Kits

Lakeview Valley Farms
Farmingdale, NY 11735
(888) 425-9113
nsitoys.com

Associations

Kansas City BBQ Society
Kansas City, MO 64121
(800) 963-5227
kcbs.us

Gas Grills

Broilmaster
Belleville, IL 62220
(800) 851-3153
broilmaster.com

Gourmet Sauces

Tennessee Gourmet
Mt. Juliet, TN 37122
(800) 360-6345
tngourmet.com

Porky's Gourmet Foods
Gallatin, TN 37066
(800) 767-5911
porkysgourmet.com

Turkey Fryers

Superb Outfitters
Belleville, IL 62220
(800) 851-3153
empirecomfort.com

Wood Chunks & Chips

Sam's Smoker Pro
Hartford, WI 53027
(262) 673-0677
samssmoker.com

Grill Pads

DiversiTech
Decatur, GA 30035
(800) 397-4823
diversitech.com

Author's Acknowledgements

When the concept for *Mastering The BBQ* was first born, the focus was going to be exclusively barbecue, not grilling, and the book would include advice and recommendations for the unskilled backyard cook. Over the years, the notion evolved to include grilling recipes because we don't always have the time to barbecue and the information was expanded to be helpful to backyard grill masters and smokers regardless of their expertise.

Thanks to the hundreds of cooks who regularly posted to cooking and recipe bulletin boards in the 1980s and 1990s, before the Internet became such a source of information. A number of the recipes in this book have been crafted from those postings and from recipes and suggestions offered by friends, co-workers, and family.

There is no such thing as a new recipe. Someone, somewhere, sometime has done it before and all a professional chef does is adapt a particular recipe to our personal style and presentation. If one searches the Internet or researches the thousands of cookbooks already published, you may find a recipe similar to one in *Mastering The BBQ* but it will be difficult to find a similar compilation and collection of proven barbecue and grilling recipes, tips, and techniques.

Special thanks to Sue Sykes at Tennessee Gourmet™ products (tngourmet.com) for her collaboration, support, cajoling, berating, encouragement, and outright nagging throughout the often-arduous process of researching, writing, revising, editing, and re-writing *Mastering The BBQ*. Thanks also to Tom Ellison for his help with graphics and layout; Sam Farrow of Sam's Smoker Pro for providing a great product to try and illustrations to use; DiversiTech for providing "The Original Grill Pad" to protect the deck and patio during the months of testing recipes and also for many of the illustrations used throughout the book; and Distinctive Culinary Concepts for its innovative ceramic grilling squares that I personally recommend. My gratitude also goes to Empire Comfort Systems, the manufacturers of Broilmaster grills, for their product illustrations; David Klose at BBQ Pits by Klose for the photographs he provided of his custom smokers and his critique of the book; and Ken's Custom BBQ Pits for the photographs they provided. Also, the Mississippi State University Extension Service, the Texas Beef Council, the National Chicken Council, the National Pork Board, and Candy Weaver, author of *Cooking With Smoke*, for their assistance and contributions to *Mastering The BBQ*. The resources page also lists other contributors. If I have overlooked anyone, please accept my apologies.

I invite your comments, suggestions, and critiques. Please e-mail me at *bbqChef@comcast.net*.

Michael H. Stines
Cape Cod, Massachusetts

About The Author:

After a successful career as a journalist, editor, and publisher, Mike Stines traded a typewriter for stainless steel tongs and worked through the stations to become executive chef at a Cape Cod restaurant specializing in barbecue and grilled foods. He is also the author of *Food With An Attitude*, a cookbook and recipe collection featuring hot and spicy cuisines from across the country.

A resident of Cape Cod, Massachusetts, he is a certified barbecue judge for the Kansas City Barbeque Society and has judged the prestigious American Royal Invitational BBQ Competition known as the "World Series of Barbecue." He is also a member of the New England Barbecue Society, the National Barbecue Association, the Greater Omaha Barbecue Society, the Lone Star Barbecue Society, the Chili Appreciation Society International, and the International Chili Society.

In the amateur division of the 2004 *Fiery-Foods & BBQ* Scovie Awards, he received a second-place finish for his "Habanero-Cranberry Jelly." Two barbecue sauce entries were awarded third and fourth place in the same competition. His "Seven-Chile Chili" was one of ten winning chili recipes in the magazine's 2003 Great Chili Contest. In the 2004 Zesty Best food competition, his "Cumberland Barbecue Sauce" received a third place award.

He is a frequent guest on *Fooding Around*, a radio talk show broadcast in southern New England highlighting trends in the hospitality industry and a regular columnist for the *National Barbecue News*, a monthly newspaper focusing on barbecue across the country, *Fiery Foods & BBQ* magazine, and other specialty barbecue and cooking publications. He also serves as the executive editor for *The BBQer* magazine, the only magazine devoted exclusively to outdoor cooking and barbecue.

Additional copies of *Mastering The BBQ* may be ordered online at **www.tngourmet.com** or by calling (800) 360-6345.